Artificial Intelligence in Healthcare

Transforming Medicine fromPrevention to Personalized Treatment

SOPHIA KANGARLU MD, FACP, CHCQM, MBA, FABQAURP.

Artificial Intelligence in Healthcare

ISBN: 979-8-2956-4088-9 (**Paperback**)

Library of Congress Control Number LCCN: 2026904793

 First printing edition 2026.

DISCLAIMER

This book is intended for informational and educational purposes only. It does not constitute medical, legal, regulatory, or professional advice of any kind. The content reflects current knowledge and practices at the time of writing, which may evolve as technology, evidence, and regulations change.

Artificial intelligence systems discussed in this book should not be relied upon as a substitute for professional clinical judgment. Healthcare decisions must always be made by qualified professionals based on individual patient circumstances.

The authors and publisher make no warranties regarding the accuracy, completeness, or applicability of the information provided. Implementation of AI in healthcare carries ethical, legal, and safety responsibilities that vary by jurisdiction.

Readers are advised to consult appropriate experts before adopting or deploying AI systems. Neither the authors nor the publisher assumes liability for outcomes arising from the use of this material.

Table of Contents

Introduction

Healthcare is undergoing a structural transformation unlike any it has experienced before. For decades, progress in medicine has been driven primarily by advances in pharmaceuticals, medical devices, and clinical protocols. While these remain critical, a new and equally powerful force has emerged, artificial intelligence (AI).

AI is reshaping how healthcare systems prevent disease, diagnose illness, deliver care, allocate resources, and engage patients across the continuum of health and disease.

At its core, healthcare is an information-intensive domain. Every patient encounter generates data: symptoms described in natural language, laboratory values, imaging scans, genomic sequences, physiological signals, and behavioral patterns. Historically, much of this data has been underutilized, fragmented across systems, or interpreted through human cognition alone. As the volume, velocity, and complexity of health data have expanded, the limitations of purely human-driven analysis have become increasingly apparent.

Artificial intelligence offers a way to transform raw data into actionable insights at scale.

The relevance of AI in healthcare extends far beyond efficiency gains. AI has the potential to enable earlier disease detection, more precise diagnoses, personalized treatment strategies, continuous monitoring of chronic conditions, and expanded access to care through virtual and remote platforms.

At the same time, it raises profound questions about ethics, equity, transparency, accountability, and the future role of healthcare professionals.

This book is designed to provide a structured, evidence-informed, and practical exploration of artificial intelligence in healthcare. It addresses not only what AI can do, but how it works, where it is most effective, and what challenges must be navigated for responsible adoption.

Rather than treating AI as a futuristic abstraction, the book focuses on real-world applications across prevention, diagnosis, treatment, monitoring, emergency care, and system-level decision-making.

Part I - Foundations establishes the conceptual groundwork. It introduces what artificial intelligence truly means in a healthcare context, traces its historical evolution in medicine, and examines why AI has become strategically essential given today's strained healthcare landscape. This section also explains the core technologies that power healthcare AI - machine learning, deep learning, natural language processing, computer vision, and predictive analytics - along with the key data sources such as electronic health records, genomics, imaging, and wearables. The goal here is to ensure readers understand not just what AI does, but how it works and what it depends on.

Part II - AI Across the Healthcare Continuum forms the core of the book and focuses on real-world applications. It explores how AI supports prevention, early detection, diagnosis, treatment, monitoring, and long-term care. This includes detailed chapters on fitness tracking and mobile health apps, symptom checkers and AI-driven triage, early disease detection, robotic and image-guided surgery, continuous disease monitoring, virtual health assistants, emergency care, telemedicine, and personalized treatment planning. Each chapter balances technical explanation with clinical relevance, highlighting both benefits and limitations, and showing how AI fits into actual care pathways rather than existing as a standalone technology.

Part III - Enablers and Challenges addresses the critical factors that determine whether AI succeeds or fails in healthcare settings. This section covers data governance, privacy, cybersecurity, interoperability, and regulatory requirements, alongside ethical, legal, and social implications, such as bias, transparency, accountability, and patient trust. It also includes a dedicated chapter on implementation strategies, covering workflow integration, workforce transformation, evaluation metrics, and responsible scaling of AI solutions within health systems.

Part IV - Future Directions looks ahead to where healthcare AI is going next. It explores emerging areas such as generative AI in clinical practice, digital twins, brain-computer interfaces, predictive public health, pandemic preparedness, and AI-driven drug discovery and clinical trials. The concluding section brings the book together by outlining what it will take to realize the promise of AI in healthcare while keeping care human-centered, ethical, and equitable.

The book offers a structured, balanced, and realistic view of AI in healthcare, one that explains the technology, demonstrates its applications, addresses its risks, and provides a roadmap for responsible adoption. It is intended to inform, guide decision-making, and support thoughtful engagement with AI rather than promote hype or oversimplified narratives.

Part I

Foundations

Chapter 1: Introduction to AI in Healthcare

Healthcare is at a pivotal moment. Advances in medical science have dramatically improved outcomes over the past century, yet health systems around the world now face unprecedented pressure from rising costs, aging populations, chronic disease burden, and increasing complexity of care.

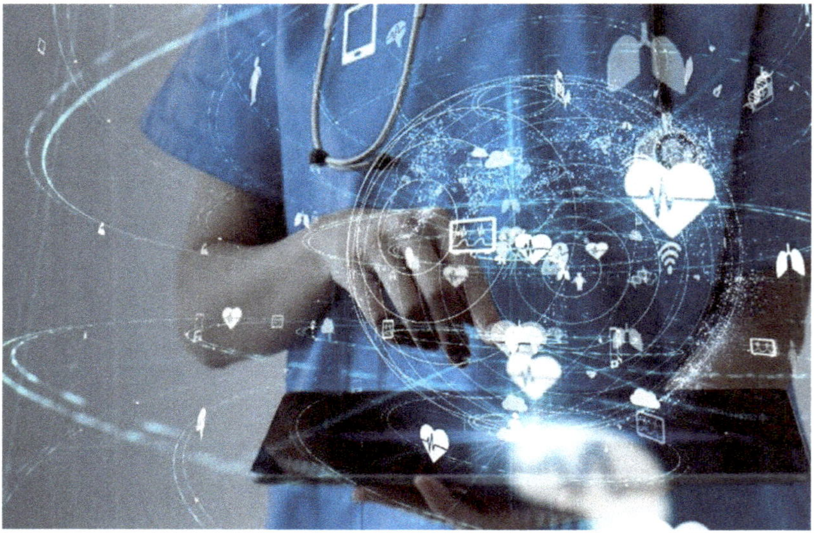

At the same time, healthcare has become one of the most data-rich industries, generating vast amounts of clinical, biological, and behavioral information with every patient interaction. Artificial intelligence has emerged at the intersection of these challenges and opportunities.

This chapter introduces artificial intelligence in the context of healthcare, clarifying what AI is and what it is not, while setting realistic expectations for its role in modern medicine. Rather than presenting AI as a futuristic replacement for clinicians, this chapter frames it as a decision-support capability designed to augment human expertise, enhance consistency, and enable more proactive and personalized care. It traces the historical evolution of AI in medicine, from early rule-based systems to today's data-driven models, and situates this evolution within the realities of today's healthcare landscape.

By examining why AI adoption has become a strategic necessity, this chapter establishes the conceptual foundation for the rest of the book. It prepares you to engage critically with AI not as hype, but as a transformative tool whose impact depends on responsible design, thoughtful integration, and human-centered use.

What Is Artificial Intelligence?

Artificial intelligence (AI) refers to the development of computer systems capable of performing tasks that traditionally require human intelligence. These tasks include learning from experience, recognizing patterns, understanding and generating language, interpreting visual information, making decisions under uncertainty, and adapting behavior based on new data.

Unlike conventional software systems, which operate according to fixed rules explicitly programmed by humans, AI systems are designed to learn and evolve as they are exposed to increasing amounts of information.

At a fundamental level, AI shifts computation from rule execution to pattern discovery.

Instead of being told exactly how to solve a problem, AI systems infer solutions by identifying relationships within data. This distinction is particularly important in healthcare, where clinical decision-making often involves complexity, ambiguity, and variability that cannot be fully captured by rigid rules.

In the healthcare context, artificial intelligence does not exist as a single, monolithic technology. Rather, it encompasses a diverse set of computational methods, including machine learning algorithms, neural networks, natural language processing systems, and predictive models. These tools are applied across clinical, administrative, operational, and research domains.

AI systems may assist clinicians by identifying abnormalities in medical images, predicting disease risk, recommending treatment pathways, monitoring patients remotely, or automating repetitive administrative tasks such as documentation and billing.

Crucially, most AI systems in healthcare are designed to be assistive rather than autonomous. Their primary function is to support human decision-making, not to replace it.

A diagnostic algorithm, for example, may highlight areas of concern on a radiology scan, but the final interpretation and clinical decision remain the responsibility of a qualified healthcare professional. This collaborative model reflects both practical realities and ethical considerations, recognizing the importance of human judgment, empathy, and accountability in medical care.

AI systems also operate across a spectrum of sophistication. At the most basic level are rule-based systems that follow predefined logic, such as alerts triggered when laboratory values exceed established thresholds. While these systems are not "intelligent" in the modern sense, they represent early forms of clinical decision support. More advanced AI systems rely on machine learning, enabling them to identify complex, nonlinear patterns within large datasets-patterns that may be difficult or impossible for humans to detect unaided.

These advanced systems can analyze vast quantities of data at speeds far exceeding human capability. They can synthesize information from multiple sources, such as electronic health records, imaging data, genomic profiles, and wearable sensors, to generate insights at both individual and population levels. This scalability is one of AI's most significant advantages in healthcare, where clinicians often face information overload.

A critical conceptual distinction in AI is between narrow AI and general AI. Narrow AI refers to systems designed to perform specific tasks within well-defined domains. Examples in healthcare include algorithms that detect diabetic retinopathy from retinal images, predict hospital readmission risk, or classify skin lesions. All AI systems currently deployed in healthcare fall into this category. They may achieve high levels of performance within their intended scope, but do not possess general reasoning or consciousness.

General AI, by contrast, would exhibit human-like intelligence across a wide range of tasks, including reasoning, abstraction, and transfer of knowledge between domains. Such systems remain theoretical and are not part of contemporary medical practice. Recognizing this distinction is important for managing expectations and ensuring realistic discussions about AI's role in healthcare.

Understanding AI in healthcare also requires acknowledging its limitations. AI systems are fundamentally dependent on the data used to train them. If training data is incomplete, biased, or unrepresentative, the resulting models may produce inaccurate or inequitable outcomes. AI systems lack intrinsic understanding, moral reasoning, and situational awareness. They do not "understand" patients in a human sense, nor can they independently weigh ethical considerations or contextual subtleties.

For these reasons, responsible AI deployment demands rigorous validation, continuous monitoring, and thoughtful integration into clinical workflows. AI should be viewed not as a replacement for human clinicians, but as a decision-support infrastructure-one that enhances consistency, efficiency, and precision while preserving human oversight and accountability.

Historical Evolution of AI in Medicine

The application of artificial intelligence to medicine has a longer history than is often assumed.

Early efforts can be traced back to the 1960s and 1970s, when researchers began exploring symbolic AI and expert systems designed to emulate human reasoning. These systems relied on explicit rules and knowledge bases created by domain experts, rather than learning from data.

One of the most notable early examples was MYCIN, a rule-based expert system developed at Stanford University to assist in diagnosing bacterial infections and recommending antibiotic treatments. MYCIN demonstrated diagnostic accuracy comparable to that of experienced clinicians and highlighted the potential of AI to support medical decision-making. However, despite its technical success, MYCIN was never widely adopted in clinical practice.

Several factors limited the early impact of AI in medicine. Computing power was constrained, making it difficult to scale systems or process large datasets. Clinical data was largely paper-based, fragmented, and inaccessible for computational analysis. Integration with clinical workflows was minimal, and concerns about legal liability, trust, and accountability further hindered adoption.

Throughout the 1980s and 1990s, AI research in medicine continued primarily within academic and experimental settings. While incremental advances were made, real-world clinical deployment remained rare. Healthcare systems lacked the digital infrastructure necessary to support data-driven AI, and the cost of computation remained high.

The modern resurgence of AI in healthcare began in the late 2000s and early 2010s, driven by several converging developments.

First, the widespread adoption of electronic health records transformed clinical data into digital formats, creating large repositories of structured and unstructured information. Second, advances in computing hardware, particularly the use of graphics processing units, have dramatically increased the feasibility of training complex machine learning models. Third, breakthroughs in deep learning significantly improved performance in tasks such as image recognition, speech processing, and natural language understanding.

These developments marked a shift from knowledge-driven AI to data-driven AI. Instead of relying on manually encoded rules, modern AI systems learn directly from examples, enabling them to capture subtle and complex patterns. In healthcare, this translated into rapid progress across medical imaging, pathology, genomics, and risk prediction.

By the mid-2010s, AI systems began demonstrating performance that rivaled or surpassed traditional statistical models and, in some cases, matched expert clinicians on narrow tasks. Algorithms showed promise in detecting cancers earlier, identifying disease progression, and supporting clinical decision-making in high-volume settings.

More recently, AI applications have expanded beyond diagnostics into broader aspects of healthcare delivery. These include remote patient monitoring, virtual health assistants, robotic and image-guided surgery, population health analytics, and personalized treatment planning.

The COVID-19 pandemic further accelerated AI adoption by exposing vulnerabilities in traditional care models and underscoring the need for scalable, data-driven solutions.

The historical evolution of AI in medicine underscores a critical insight: technological capability alone does not guarantee impact. Successful adoption depends on alignment with clinical needs, regulatory frameworks, ethical principles, and organizational readiness. This lesson continues to shape contemporary discussions about AI implementation in healthcare.

The Healthcare Landscape Today

Modern healthcare systems operate within an environment of unprecedented complexity and pressure. Demographic shifts, particularly aging populations, have increased demand for healthcare services while straining existing resources. Chronic diseases such as diabetes, cardiovascular disease, and cancer account for a growing share of morbidity and healthcare expenditure, requiring long-term management rather than episodic care.

At the same time, healthcare workforces face significant challenges. Many regions experience shortages of physicians, nurses, and allied health professionals, while clinicians who remain in practice contend with increasing administrative burdens. Documentation requirements, regulatory compliance, and fragmented digital systems contribute to burnout and reduced job satisfaction.

Patients, meanwhile, have evolving expectations. They increasingly demand timely access, personalized care, transparency, and digital engagement. Yet many experience fragmented care journeys, long wait times, and limited coordination across providers. Inequities in access and outcomes persist across socioeconomic, geographic, and demographic lines.

Compounding these challenges is the exponential growth of healthcare data. Advances in medical imaging, genomic sequencing, wearable technologies, and mobile health applications generate continuous streams of information. While this data holds enormous potential to improve diagnosis, treatment, and prevention, it also overwhelms traditional methods of analysis. Clinicians often lack the time or tools to synthesize all available information during patient encounters.

Variability in care delivery further complicates the landscape. Clinical practice differs across institutions and individual providers, leading to inconsistent outcomes. Although evidence-based guidelines exist, translating research into routine practice remains difficult, and adherence varies widely.

Digital health technologies have attempted to address some of these issues. Electronic health records have improved data availability and continuity, but have also introduced new challenges related to usability and workflow disruption. Telemedicine has expanded access in some contexts but remains unevenly implemented.

Within this complex environment, artificial intelligence emerges as a potential integrative force. By analyzing large, heterogeneous datasets, AI systems can identify patterns that support earlier intervention, reduce unwarranted variation, and enhance efficiency. AI offers tools to manage complexity at scale, enabling more proactive, coordinated, and personalized care.

However, the current landscape of AI adoption is uneven. Well-resourced institutions and technology-forward health systems are advancing rapidly, while others face barriers related to infrastructure, funding, expertise, and trust. Bridging this divide is essential to ensuring that AI contributes to improved health outcomes rather than exacerbating existing disparities.

Strategic Importance of AI Adoption in Health Systems

The adoption of artificial intelligence is no longer a discretionary innovation for healthcare systems; it has become a strategic imperative. Health systems that fail to integrate AI risk falling behind in quality, efficiency, and sustainability.

From a clinical perspective, AI enables more precise and timely decision-making. Predictive models can identify disease risk before symptoms manifest, enabling earlier intervention. Diagnostic algorithms can reduce errors and variability, particularly in high-pressure or resource-constrained environments. Personalized treatment recommendations can improve outcomes while minimizing unnecessary or ineffective interventions.

Operationally, AI offers powerful tools for optimizing healthcare delivery. Predictive analytics can anticipate patient demand, improve capacity planning, and reduce overcrowding in emergency departments. AI-driven automation can streamline scheduling, billing, and documentation, freeing clinicians to focus on direct patient care.

At the population health level, AI supports risk stratification, outbreak detection, and targeted interventions. By integrating clinical data with social and environmental factors, AI systems can help address social determinants of health and improve long-term outcomes across communities.

Strategically, AI adoption also affects competitiveness and reputation. Patients increasingly expect digital, personalized, and accessible care experiences. Payers and regulators demand evidence of quality, safety, and cost-effectiveness. Health systems that leverage AI effectively are better positioned to meet these expectations and adapt to evolving policy and market conditions.

However, realizing these benefits requires more than technological investment. Strategic AI adoption demands robust governance structures, workforce training, ethical oversight, and cultural change. Organizations must move beyond isolated pilot projects toward scalable, evidence-based implementation. Trust among clinicians, patients, and the public must be earned through transparency, accountability, and demonstrated value.

In this context, artificial intelligence should be understood not as a standalone solution, but as a foundational capability that reshapes how healthcare systems learn, adapt, and deliver care. The chapters that follow explore how this capability is being applied across the healthcare continuum and what is required to harness its potential responsibly.

Conclusion

Artificial intelligence has emerged as a defining force in the transformation of modern healthcare, not as a replacement for human expertise, but as a powerful extension of it.

As this chapter has shown, AI represents a shift from rigid, rule-based systems toward adaptive, data-driven approaches capable of managing the complexity, scale, and variability inherent in healthcare. From its early roots in symbolic expert systems to today's data-intensive, learning-based models, AI's evolution reflects both technological progress and the growing demands placed on health systems worldwide.

Equally important is the context in which AI is being adopted. Healthcare today faces mounting pressures from aging populations, chronic disease burden, workforce shortages, and information overload. In this environment, AI offers tools to support earlier detection, more consistent decision-making, and more proactive, personalized care. Yet its promise is inseparable from its limitations. AI systems depend on data quality, thoughtful design, and human oversight, and they raise critical questions around bias, accountability, trust, and ethics.

This chapter establishes a foundational understanding of what AI is, how it has developed within medicine, and why its adoption has become strategically essential. With this conceptual grounding in place, the focus now turns to the technologies that make healthcare AI possible, how these systems work, what data they rely on, and how they translate theory into practice.

Chapter 2: Core Technologies and Concepts

To understand how artificial intelligence transforms healthcare, it is essential to understand the technologies that power it. AI is not a single system or application, but a collection of computational approaches that work together to analyze data, recognize patterns, and support decision-making at scale.

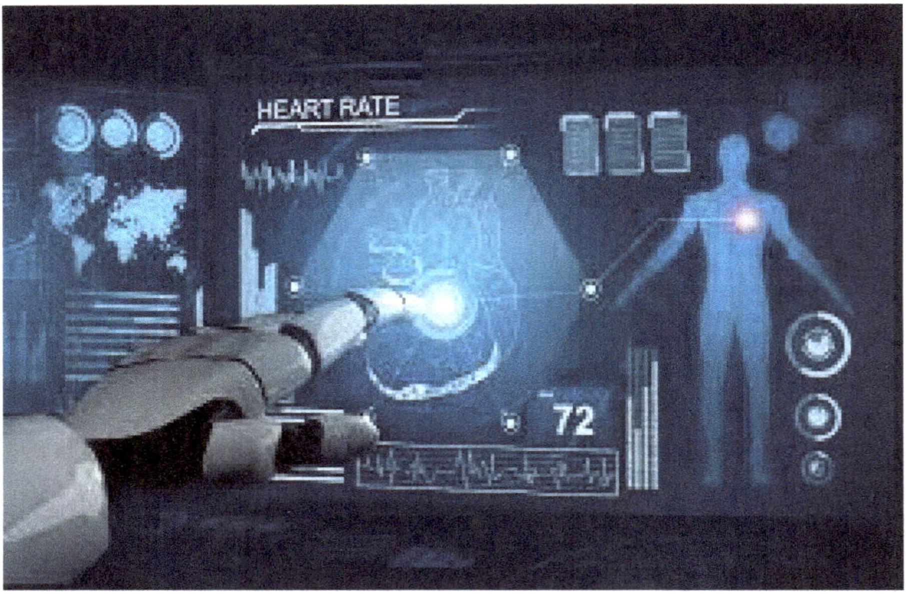

This chapter introduces the core technologies and concepts that form the technical backbone of healthcare AI. It explores machine learning and its major paradigms, including supervised, unsupervised, and reinforcement learning, alongside deep learning and neural networks that enable complex pattern recognition in images, genomics, and clinical data. It also examines natural language processing, which unlocks insight from unstructured medical text, computer vision, which scales visual interpretation in medical imaging, and predictive analytics, which supports anticipatory and preventive care.

This chapter also highlights the data sources that make these technologies viable, including electronic health records, medical images, genomic data, and wearable devices.

By establishing a clear, accessible understanding of how these technologies work and what they depend on, this chapter provides the technical foundation necessary to evaluate real-world AI applications explored in later chapters.

Machine Learning: Supervised, Unsupervised, and Reinforcement Learning

Machine learning forms the computational backbone of most artificial intelligence applications in healthcare. At its essence, machine learning refers to a class of algorithms that enable computer systems to learn from data, identify patterns, and make predictions or decisions without being explicitly programmed for every scenario.

Unlike traditional rule-based software, which follows static instructions written by developers, machine learning systems improve their performance over time as they are exposed to larger and more diverse datasets.

Healthcare is uniquely suited to machine learning because it generates enormous volumes of complex data. Clinical encounters, laboratory tests, medical images, genomic sequences, and patient-generated health data collectively create a rich environment for algorithmic learning.

However, the way a machine learning model learns depends heavily on how the data is structured and what kind of problem is being addressed.

Broadly, machine learning approaches in healthcare are categorized into supervised learning, unsupervised learning, and reinforcement learning.

Supervised Learning in Healthcare

Supervised learning is the most widely used machine learning approach in healthcare today.

In supervised learning, algorithms are trained on labeled datasets, meaning that each input example is paired with a known output or outcome. The model's objective is to learn a mapping between inputs and outputs so that it can accurately predict outcomes for new, unseen data.

In a healthcare context, supervised learning is commonly used for diagnostic classification, risk prediction, and outcome forecasting. For example, a model might be trained on historical patient records where the presence or absence of a disease is known. The inputs may include demographic data, laboratory values, imaging features, and clinical history, while the output is a diagnosis, risk score, or probability estimate.

One of the major strengths of supervised learning is its relative interpretability, particularly when using simpler models such as logistic regression or decision trees. Clinicians and regulators often prefer models that can provide explanations for their predictions, especially when those predictions influence medical decisions.

As a result, supervised learning has become a cornerstone of clinical decision support systems, early warning scores, and screening tools.

However, supervised learning also has limitations. It requires large volumes of high-quality labeled data, which can be expensive and time-consuming to obtain in healthcare. Labeling medical data often requires expert clinicians, and inconsistencies in diagnosis or documentation can introduce noise.

Additionally, supervised models tend to perform best within the specific population and context in which they were trained, raising concerns about generalizability and bias when applied across diverse patient groups.

Unsupervised Learning in Healthcare

Unsupervised learning differs fundamentally from supervised learning in that it does not rely on labeled outcomes. Instead, it seeks to identify underlying structures, patterns, or relationships within unlabeled data.

In healthcare, unsupervised learning is particularly valuable for exploratory analysis, hypothesis generation, and understanding complex disease heterogeneity.

One common application of unsupervised learning is patient clustering. By analyzing patterns across clinical variables, algorithms can group patients with similar characteristics or disease trajectories. These clusters may reveal subtypes of diseases that are not captured by traditional diagnostic categories.

For example, patients diagnosed with the same condition may exhibit distinct symptom profiles, responses to treatment, or risk factors, suggesting the need for more personalized care strategies.

Unsupervised learning is also used in anomaly detection, where the goal is to identify data points that deviate significantly from the norm. In healthcare, this can support early detection of rare conditions, identification of unusual laboratory results, or monitoring of system performance to detect errors or safety risks.

While unsupervised learning offers powerful insights, it also presents interpretability challenges. The patterns identified by these models do not inherently carry clinical meaning and must be interpreted carefully by domain experts. Without a clinical context, there is a risk of drawing incorrect conclusions or overfitting patterns that lack real-world significance.

Reinforcement Learning in Healthcare

Reinforcement learning represents a more dynamic approach to machine learning, focusing on sequential decision-making over time.

In reinforcement learning, an agent interacts with an environment, takes actions, and receives feedback in the form of rewards or penalties. The agent's objective is to learn an optimal strategy, or policy, that maximizes cumulative reward.

In healthcare, reinforcement learning is particularly promising for treatment optimization and adaptive decision-making. Many clinical decisions are not one-time events but involve a series of choices over time, such as adjusting medication dosages, selecting treatment pathways, or managing chronic diseases.

Reinforcement learning can model these scenarios by considering both immediate and long-term outcomes.

For example, reinforcement learning has been explored in optimizing insulin dosing for diabetes management, tailoring cancer treatment regimens, and managing mechanical ventilation in intensive care units. These applications aim to balance competing objectives, such as maximizing therapeutic benefit while minimizing adverse effects.

Despite its potential, reinforcement learning faces significant barriers to clinical adoption.

Training such models often requires simulated environments or retrospective data, as real-world trial-and-error learning may pose unacceptable risks to patients. Ethical considerations, safety constraints, and regulatory oversight are particularly critical when deploying reinforcement learning systems in healthcare.

Choosing the Right Approach

Each machine learning paradigm offers distinct advantages and trade-offs. Supervised learning excels in prediction and classification when labeled data is available. Unsupervised learning is invaluable for discovery and pattern recognition in complex datasets. Reinforcement learning addresses longitudinal decision-making but requires careful design and validation.

The choice of approach depends on the clinical question, data quality, available infrastructure, and acceptable risk. In practice, many healthcare AI systems combine elements of multiple learning paradigms to achieve robust and clinically meaningful performance.

Deep Learning and Neural Networks

Deep learning is a specialized subset of machine learning that uses artificial neural networks with multiple layers to model complex, nonlinear relationships in data. Inspired loosely by the structure of the human brain, neural networks consist of interconnected nodes, or neurons, that process information through weighted connections.

The defining feature of deep learning is its ability to learn hierarchical representations of data automatically.

Lower layers capture simple patterns, while deeper layers extract increasingly abstract features. This capability makes deep learning particularly effective for high-dimensional data such as medical images, genomic sequences, audio signals, and free-text clinical notes.

Deep Learning in Medical Imaging

One of the most transformative applications of deep learning in healthcare has been in medical imaging. Convolutional neural networks are designed to process visual data and have demonstrated remarkable accuracy in tasks such as detecting tumors, identifying fractures, grading disease severity, and segmenting anatomical structures.

In radiology and pathology, deep learning systems can analyze thousands of images rapidly, assisting clinicians by flagging high-risk cases, reducing diagnostic variability, and improving workflow efficiency. These systems do not replace human experts but act as second readers or triage tools, enhancing consistency and throughput.

Deep Learning in Genomics and Precision Medicine

Deep learning has also advanced the field of genomics by enabling analysis of vast genetic datasets. Neural networks can identify complex patterns in DNA sequences, gene expression profiles, and epigenetic markers that are associated with disease risk or treatment response.

In precision medicine, deep learning models support patient stratification and therapeutic targeting by integrating genomic data with clinical and environmental information. This approach moves healthcare toward more individualized treatment strategies based on biological and molecular characteristics.

Challenges of Deep Learning in Healthcare

Despite its power, deep learning presents several challenges. These models typically require large datasets and significant computational resources. More importantly, they are often criticized as "black boxes," as their internal decision-making processes are difficult to interpret.

In healthcare, where accountability and trust are paramount, this lack of transparency can hinder adoption. Clinicians may be reluctant to rely on recommendations they cannot explain to patients or justify to regulators. As a result, there is growing emphasis on explainable AI techniques that aim to make deep learning models more transparent and clinically interpretable.

Natural Language Processing

Natural language processing (NLP) enables computers to understand, interpret, and generate human language.

In healthcare, NLP is especially important because a substantial portion of clinical information exists in unstructured text. Physician notes, discharge summaries, referral letters, and patient communications contain rich clinical detail that is not easily captured in structured fields.

Applications of NLP in Healthcare

NLP systems can extract meaningful information from text, such as diagnoses, symptoms, medications, and social determinants of health. This capability supports applications including automated clinical coding, quality reporting, adverse event detection, and research data abstraction.

NLP also underpins conversational interfaces such as virtual health assistants and chatbots. These systems interact with patients using natural language, providing health education, symptom assessment, appointment scheduling, and medication reminders.

Advances and Limitations

Recent advances in NLP have significantly improved contextual understanding, enabling systems to handle medical terminology, abbreviations, and nuanced language. However, challenges remain, including ambiguity, variability in documentation styles, and the need for domain-specific training.

Ensuring accuracy and minimizing misinterpretation are critical, particularly when NLP outputs influence clinical decisions. As such, NLP systems are typically used as assistive tools rather than autonomous decision-makers.

Computer Vision

Computer vision focuses on enabling machines to interpret and analyze visual data. In healthcare, computer vision is most commonly applied to medical imaging, but its scope extends to areas such as surgical video analysis, dermatological assessment, and monitoring of patient movement and behavior.

Computer vision algorithms identify patterns, classify abnormalities, and quantify changes over time. These capabilities support early diagnosis, disease staging, and treatment monitoring. By automating repetitive visual analysis tasks, computer vision helps address workforce shortages and large imaging volumes.

As imaging data continues to grow, computer vision will play a central role in maintaining diagnostic quality while improving efficiency.

Predictive Analytics

Predictive analytics uses historical and real-time data to forecast future events or outcomes.

In healthcare, predictive models support proactive decision-making by identifying patients at risk, anticipating resource needs, and guiding preventive interventions.

Applications include predicting hospital readmissions, identifying patients at risk of deterioration, forecasting disease outbreaks, and optimizing care pathways. Predictive analytics enables a shift from reactive care to preventive and anticipatory models of healthcare delivery.

Successful implementation requires high-quality data, rigorous validation, and integration into clinical workflows. When these conditions are met, predictive analytics can improve outcomes while reducing costs and inefficiencies.

Data Sources: EHR, Genomics, Images, and Wearables

AI systems in healthcare rely on diverse data sources.

For example, electronic health records provide longitudinal clinical data, including diagnoses, treatments, and outcomes. Genomic data offers molecular-level insights into disease mechanisms. Medical imaging supplies visual representations of anatomy and pathology. Wearables and mobile devices contribute continuous data on physiology and behavior.

Integrating these data sources remains a major challenge due to interoperability issues, variable data quality, and governance constraints. However, such integration is essential for holistic, patient-centered AI systems that support personalized and preventive care.

Addressing these challenges requires robust data standards, ethical governance frameworks, and collaboration across stakeholders.

Conclusion

The technologies explored in this chapter form the technical foundation upon which all healthcare AI applications are built.

Machine learning enables systems to learn from clinical data, deep learning unlocks complex pattern recognition in images and genomics, natural language processing transforms unstructured clinical text into usable information, computer vision scales visual interpretation, and predictive analytics supports proactive, forward-looking care.

Together, these approaches allow healthcare systems to move beyond isolated data points toward integrated, actionable intelligence.

At the same time, this chapter highlights that no single technology operates in isolation.

Effective healthcare AI depends on the thoughtful combination of learning paradigms, aligned with clearly defined clinical objectives and supported by high-quality, interoperable data. The diversity of data sources, such as electronic health records, medical images, genomic data, and wearables, creates enormous opportunities, but also introduces challenges related to integration, governance, and reliability.

Understanding these core technologies is essential not only for technical accuracy but for responsible adoption. Their strengths, limitations, and trade-offs directly shape how AI performs in real-world healthcare settings.

Part II

AI Across the Healthcare Continuum

Chapter 3: AI for Health and Fitness Tracking

The shift from episodic healthcare to continuous health management represents one of the most significant changes in modern medicine.

Traditionally, healthcare systems have focused on diagnosing and treating disease once symptoms become apparent. However, many of today's most pressing health challenges, such as obesity, cardiovascular disease, diabetes, and metabolic disorders, develop gradually over time and are strongly influenced by daily behaviors.

Artificial intelligence has emerged as a critical enabler in addressing this gap by supporting continuous health and fitness tracking outside traditional clinical settings.

AI-powered health and fitness tracking systems extend care beyond hospitals and clinics into everyday life. Through wearables, mobile applications, and connected devices, these systems collect real-time data on physical activity, sleep, heart rate, nutrition, stress, and other behavioral and physiological indicators. AI algorithms analyze this data to identify patterns, assess risk, and deliver personalized feedback aimed at supporting healthier behaviors and early intervention.

This chapter explores how AI is applied in health and fitness tracking, beginning with the role of wearables and mobile applications, followed by intelligent activity recognition, personalized alerts and behavioral coaching, integration of lifestyle data into medical records, and the challenges that must be addressed to ensure accuracy, engagement, and privacy.

Wearables and Mobile Apps

Wearable devices and mobile health applications form the technological backbone of AI-driven health and fitness tracking. Together, they act as the primary interface between individuals and digital health ecosystems, enabling continuous data collection beyond traditional clinical environments.

Unlike episodic measurements obtained during healthcare visits, wearables capture real-world, longitudinal data that reflects how people move, sleep, recover, and respond to daily stressors. Mobile applications serve as the connective layer, transforming sensor outputs into interpretable information and facilitating communication between users, healthcare providers, and digital care platforms.

Common wearable devices include smartwatches, fitness bands, chest straps, smart rings, and increasingly, sensor-embedded clothing and footwear. These devices are designed to be worn consistently, allowing for passive data collection without disrupting daily activities.

Mobile health applications complement wearables by functioning as dashboards, analytics engines, and engagement tools. They display trends, generate insights, deliver alerts, and often integrate educational or coaching features that encourage sustained use.

Modern wearables are equipped with a range of sensors that enable increasingly sophisticated health monitoring. Accelerometers and gyroscopes measure movement and orientation, allowing devices to detect activity type, intensity, and posture. Photoplethysmography sensors estimate heart rate and heart rate variability by analyzing changes in blood flow, while temperature sensors track peripheral or skin temperature trends.

Some advanced wearables include electrocardiogram sensors capable of capturing single-lead ECG data, enabling detection of certain cardiac irregularities. These sensors generate high-frequency data streams that reflect both behavioral and physiological states.

Mobile applications play a critical role in managing this data. They aggregate sensor inputs, apply preprocessing to reduce noise, store information securely, and present users with summaries and visualizations. Without artificial intelligence, however, the value of this data would remain limited. Raw sensor outputs are often overwhelming, fragmented, and difficult to interpret without advanced analytics.

Artificial intelligence significantly enhances the utility of wearables and mobile apps by transforming raw data into actionable health insights. Rather than simply reporting metrics such as step counts or average heart rate, AI systems analyze patterns over time, account for contextual factors, and infer higher-level health states.

For example, machine learning models can distinguish between walking, running, cycling, strength training, and sedentary behavior based on subtle differences in movement signals. AI can also infer sleep stages, estimate recovery quality, and identify deviations from an individual's baseline.

A particularly impactful application of AI is the detection of anomalies.

By learning an individual's normal physiological patterns, AI systems can identify unusual changes that may warrant attention. Irregular heart rhythms, sustained elevations in resting heart rate, or unexpected declines in activity can serve as early indicators of illness, overtraining, or disease exacerbation.

In some cases, these insights prompt users to seek medical evaluation earlier than they otherwise might.

From a healthcare perspective, wearables and mobile apps play an increasingly important role in preventive care and chronic disease management. Continuous monitoring allows for early identification of unhealthy trends, such as declining activity levels, disrupted sleep, or increasing physiological stress.

Over time, these signals can inform interventions aimed at preventing disease progression rather than reacting to acute events.

For patients managing chronic conditions, wearable data offers valuable context that traditional clinical measurements often miss. Patients with diabetes, for example, may use activity and sleep data alongside glucose monitoring to understand how lifestyle factors influence glycemic control. For those with hypertension or cardiovascular disease, trends in activity, heart rate variability, and recovery can provide insight into treatment adherence, physical conditioning, and potential triggers for symptom worsening.

Clinicians reviewing this data gain a more comprehensive view of patient behavior between visits, supporting more personalized and informed care decisions.

At a population level, aggregated wearable data can support public health initiatives and research. AI-driven analysis of anonymized datasets can reveal behavioral trends, identify risk patterns, and inform preventive strategies.

However, such use must be governed carefully to ensure ethical data use and protect individual privacy.

Despite their promise, the widespread adoption of wearables introduces important challenges related to data quality and consistency. Consumer-grade devices vary significantly in sensor accuracy, calibration, sampling rates, and data standards. Measurements may be affected by device placement, user behavior, skin tone, body composition, and environmental conditions.

As a result, AI models must be designed to handle noisy, incomplete, and heterogeneous data.

Robust AI systems address these challenges through personalization and continuous learning. Rather than relying on universal thresholds, models adapt to individual baselines and adjust for known sources of variability. Validation against clinical-grade measurements is essential, particularly when wearable data informs medical decisions. Transparency about limitations and appropriate use cases is equally important to prevent overinterpretation or misuse.

Ultimately, wearables and mobile apps represent a powerful entry point for AI-enabled healthcare. When combined with thoughtful design, rigorous validation, and responsible integration into healthcare systems, they enable a shift from episodic measurement to continuous insight, laying the foundation for more proactive, personalized, and preventive models of care.

Intelligent Activity Recognition

One of the most significant contributions of artificial intelligence to health and fitness tracking is intelligent activity recognition.

Activity recognition refers to the automated identification of physical activities and behaviors using data generated by wearable sensors. While early fitness trackers relied on simple rule-based thresholds, such as counting steps based on repetitive motion, modern AI systems employ machine learning models capable of recognizing a wide range of activities with far greater accuracy, adaptability, and contextual understanding.

These systems analyze complex patterns in motion data, including acceleration, orientation, frequency, and variability, to classify activities such as walking, running, cycling, climbing stairs, strength training, and sedentary behavior.

By examining how these signals change over time, AI models can distinguish between similar movements that would otherwise be difficult to separate using traditional methods.

For example, walking uphill produces a different motion and physiological signature than walking on flat ground, and AI can account for such differences when estimating exertion and workload.

More advanced activity recognition models go beyond static classification to identify transitions between activities and changes in intensity. They can detect when a person moves from sitting to standing, begins exercising after a period of inactivity, or shifts from moderate to vigorous effort.

Contextual factors such as posture, cadence, and environmental conditions may also be inferred, improving the accuracy of activity interpretation in real-world settings.

AI-driven recognition is not limited to physical movement alone. By integrating heart rate, heart rate variability, and time-of-day data, activity recognition systems can assess sedentary behavior, recovery states, and even physiological stress. Sleep analysis is a prominent example. AI models infer sleep duration, stages, and quality by combining subtle movement patterns with cardiovascular signals. These insights help identify sleep disturbances, irregular schedules, or insufficient recovery, all of which are closely linked to metabolic health, immune function, and mental well-being.

Accurate activity recognition also enables more precise estimation of energy expenditure. Rather than applying generic formulas based solely on step counts or body weight, AI models personalize calorie burn estimates by accounting for activity type, intensity, individual physiology, and historical patterns.

This personalization improves the relevance of feedback provided to users and supports more effective fitness planning and weight management.

From a clinical perspective, intelligent activity recognition offers objective measures of functional status. For older adults, reduced mobility or changes in gait patterns may signal increased fall risk or early functional decline. For patients recovering from surgery or managing chronic conditions, gradual improvements or setbacks in daily activity can provide valuable insight into recovery progress.

AI systems can detect subtle, longitudinal changes that may not be evident during brief clinical encounters.

Despite its advantages, activity recognition remains technically challenging. Human movement is highly variable and influenced by context, lifestyle, and environment. Models trained in controlled laboratory settings may perform differently in everyday life.

Ensuring reliability, therefore, requires diverse training datasets, continuous refinement, and validation across populations. When implemented thoughtfully, intelligent activity recognition becomes a powerful tool for both personal health management and clinical insight.

Personalized Alerts and Behavioral Coaching

Data collection alone does not lead to meaningful health improvement. The true impact of AI-driven health and fitness tracking emerges when data is translated into timely, relevant, and personalized interventions that support behavior change. Personalized alerts and behavioral coaching represent one of the most influential applications of artificial intelligence in this domain, bridging the gap between insight and action.

AI systems continuously analyze individual data patterns, such as activity levels, sleep quality, physiological responses, and historical trends, to determine when and how to intervene. Unlike generic reminders or static recommendations, personalized alerts are tailored to an individual's habits, preferences, goals, and risk profile.

For example, an AI system may recognize that a user tends to become sedentary in the late afternoon and deliver a brief movement prompt at that specific time, rather than issuing a blanket daily reminder.

Similarly, for individuals engaged in structured exercise, AI can detect periods of excessive training load and recommend rest or recovery-focused activities to reduce injury risk.

Behavioral coaching systems often incorporate principles from behavioral science, including goal setting, habit formation, reinforcement, and self-efficacy. AI enables these principles to be applied dynamically. Goals can be adjusted automatically based on performance, feedback can be framed positively to reinforce progress, and interventions can be modified when engagement declines.

Over time, the system learns which strategies resonate most with each individual, refining its approach to maximize adherence and long-term behavior change.

In healthcare settings, personalized alerts play a valuable role in disease prevention and chronic condition management. For individuals at elevated risk of cardiovascular disease, AI systems may monitor activity patterns, sleep consistency, and stress indicators to provide early lifestyle recommendations or prompt preventive action. For patients managing conditions such as diabetes, hypertension, or obesity, alerts can reinforce adherence to physical activity goals, medication schedules, or dietary plans, helping to reduce complications and improve outcomes.

AI-driven behavioral coaching also extends to mental and emotional well-being.

By analyzing physiological signals such as heart rate variability alongside behavioral patterns, systems can identify periods of elevated stress or fatigue. In response, they may suggest coping strategies such as breathing exercises, mindfulness sessions, sleep optimization, or reduced training intensity. These interventions support a more holistic approach to health that recognizes the interconnection between physical and mental states.

However, personalization must be implemented carefully to maintain user trust and autonomy.

Excessive alerts, poorly timed messages, or overly prescriptive recommendations can lead to disengagement, frustration, or alert fatigue. Effective AI coaching systems prioritize relevance and transparency, clearly explaining why an alert is triggered and allowing users to customize goals, notification frequency, and intervention types.

When designed thoughtfully, personalized alerts and behavioral coaching transform passive data collection into an active partnership that empowers individuals to make sustainable health decisions.

Integrating Lifestyle Data with Medical Records

One of the most promising, yet technically and organizationally complex, developments in AI-driven health tracking is the integration of lifestyle data into formal healthcare systems.

Traditionally, clinical decision-making has been based on episodic data collected during scheduled encounters, such as laboratory results, imaging studies, and physical examinations. While these data points are clinically valuable, they offer only a snapshot of a patient's health.

Wearables and mobile health applications introduce a continuous stream of real-world data that reflects how individuals live, move, sleep, and recover between clinical visits.

Artificial intelligence plays a central role in making this volume of lifestyle data usable in clinical settings. Raw sensor data is typically high-frequency, noisy, and impractical for direct review by clinicians. AI systems filter, aggregate, and contextualize this information, transforming it into concise summaries, trend analyses, and clinically meaningful alerts.

For example, sustained declines in physical activity, increasing sleep fragmentation, or rising physiological stress levels may indicate worsening disease control, early illness, or reduced treatment adherence.

Conversely, gradual improvements in these metrics may reflect successful lifestyle interventions or effective treatment adjustments.

Integrating lifestyle data into electronic health records supports a more holistic and patient-centered approach to care. When combined with traditional clinical data, lifestyle metrics provide insight into behavioral and environmental factors that strongly influence health outcomes.

This integration is particularly valuable in chronic disease management, where long-term behavior change is often as important as medication.

For patients with diabetes, for example, trends in activity, sleep, and recovery can help clinicians contextualize glucose fluctuations and tailor treatment recommendations. In cardiovascular care, wearable-derived activity and heart rate data can inform exercise prescriptions and risk assessments.

Beyond individual care, aggregated lifestyle data has significant value at the population level.

AI systems can analyze anonymized datasets to identify patterns associated with disease onset, progression, or response to intervention.

These insights can inform preventive care strategies, support risk stratification, and guide resource allocation.

For example, identifying communities with declining activity levels or poor sleep patterns may help target public health interventions or wellness programs before disease prevalence increases.

Despite its potential, integrating lifestyle data into medical records presents several challenges.

Interoperability remains a major barrier, as wearable platforms, mobile apps, and health record systems often use different data standards and formats. Clinical workflow alignment is equally important; data must be presented in ways that support, rather than disrupt, decision-making. Reimbursement models also influence adoption, as clinicians need clear incentives and guidelines for using lifestyle data in care delivery.

Finally, trust is essential. Clinicians must have confidence in the accuracy, relevance, and limitations of wearable data, and patients must understand how their information is used. Clear governance frameworks, validation standards, and transparent communication are critical to ensuring that lifestyle data integration enhances care rather than adding complexity or uncertainty.

Challenges: Accuracy, Engagement, and Data Privacy

Despite the growing adoption of AI-driven health and fitness tracking, significant challenges remain that must be addressed to ensure these systems are effective, trustworthy, and equitable. Accuracy, sustained user engagement, and data privacy are among the most critical concerns shaping both individual outcomes and broader healthcare integration.

Accuracy remains a foundational issue. Most wearable devices used for health tracking are consumer-grade products, and their sensor quality, calibration, and performance vary widely across manufacturers and models. Numerous factors, including skin tone, body composition, wrist placement, movement artifacts, and ambient conditions such as temperature and lighting, can influence measurements of heart rate, sleep stages, and energy expenditure. For example, photoplethysmography-based heart rate sensors may perform differently in people with darker skin tones or during high-intensity exercise, leading to inconsistent readings.

AI algorithms can mitigate some of these limitations by learning individual baselines and adapting to user-specific patterns. However, this requires large, diverse training datasets and continuous validation across populations. Models trained in narrow demographic groups may perform poorly when deployed more broadly, introducing bias and reducing reliability.

In healthcare contexts, inaccurate data can lead to inappropriate recommendations or misplaced confidence, underscoring the importance of transparency around limitations and appropriate use cases.

User engagement represents an equally significant challenge. While many individuals initially adopt wearables and health apps with enthusiasm, long-term adherence often declines. Users may become disengaged if insights feel repetitive, alerts are poorly timed, or recommendations do not align with personal goals or daily realities.

For example, a system that repeatedly prompts physical activity without accounting for injury, illness, or caregiving responsibilities may frustrate users rather than motivate them.

Artificial intelligence offers tools to improve engagement by personalizing content, dynamically adjusting goals, and learning from user behavior. Systems that recognize patterns of disengagement can modify intervention frequency or delivery style to reduce fatigue. However, engagement is influenced not only by personalization but also by usability, clarity, and perceived value. If users do not understand how insights are generated or why recommendations matter, even highly sophisticated AI systems may fail to sustain interest.

Data privacy and security are particularly sensitive in the context of health tracking. Wearables and mobile apps collect detailed information about daily routines, physiological states, and sometimes location or social behavior. This data, if misused or inadequately protected, can expose users to discrimination, surveillance, or loss of trust. Ensuring informed consent, secure data storage, and strict access controls is essential.

AI systems must comply with data protection regulations and clearly communicate how data is collected, processed, and shared. Users should understand whether their data is used solely for personal insights, shared with healthcare providers, or aggregated for research or commercial purposes. Transparency and user control, such as the ability to opt in or out of data sharing, are central to maintaining trust.

Equity considerations further complicate these challenges. Access to wearable technology and digital health tools is uneven, shaped by socioeconomic status, geography, and digital literacy. Populations most likely to benefit from preventive health interventions may also face the greatest barriers to access. Without deliberate design choices, AI-driven health tracking risks widening existing health disparities by primarily serving those with greater resources and technical familiarity.

Addressing these challenges requires collaboration across disciplines.

Technologists, clinicians, policymakers, and users must work together to establish validation standards, ethical governance frameworks, and inclusive design practices. Only by confronting issues of accuracy, engagement, privacy, and equity can AI-driven health tracking move beyond novelty and become a trusted component of modern healthcare.

Conclusion

AI-powered health and fitness tracking represents a critical step toward more proactive, preventive, and personalized healthcare.

By enabling continuous monitoring, intelligent activity recognition, and personalized coaching, these systems extend care beyond clinical settings and empower individuals to take an active role in their health. When integrated responsibly into healthcare systems, lifestyle data can enrich clinical decision-making and support long-term disease prevention.

However, realizing this potential requires careful attention to accuracy, engagement, privacy, and equity. AI-driven tracking is not a standalone solution, but a foundational component of a broader shift toward data-informed, human-centered care.

The same principles underpin AI applications across diagnosis, treatment, monitoring, and system-level decision-making throughout the healthcare continuum.

Chapter 4: Symptom Checkers and AI-Driven Triage

One of the most visible and widely adopted applications of artificial intelligence in healthcare is the use of AI-powered symptom checkers and triage tools. These systems are often a patient's first point of interaction with digital healthcare, shaping decisions about whether to seek care, where to seek it, and how urgently.

As healthcare systems face growing demand, limited clinician availability, and rising costs, symptom checkers have emerged as a scalable way to guide patients through initial assessment and care navigation.

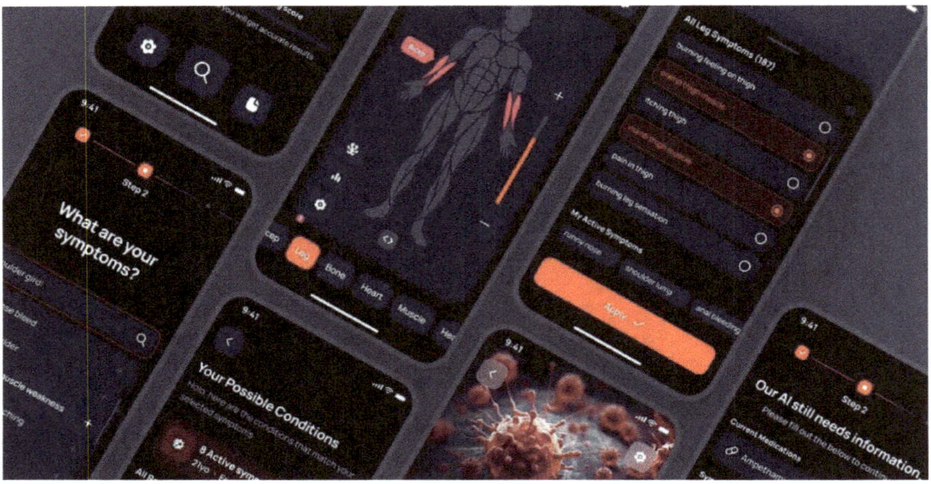

Symptoms are subjective, often vague, and influenced by context, health literacy, and emotional state. A headache, for example, may represent dehydration, stress, infection, or a serious neurological condition.

Human clinicians rely on training, experience, and intuition to evaluate such uncertainty. AI-driven systems attempt to replicate parts of this reasoning process using probabilistic models, pattern recognition, and decision logic.

This chapter examines how artificial intelligence is used to interpret symptoms, support patient decision-making, and assist triage across healthcare settings. It explores the distinction between patient-facing self-assessment tools and clinically integrated triage systems, evaluates performance and safety considerations, and addresses the critical role of user experience and health literacy in determining real-world impact.

Use of AI for Symptom Interpretation

Symptom interpretation sits at the core of AI-driven triage and represents one of the most demanding applications of artificial intelligence in healthcare.

At a basic level, symptom checkers collect information about what a person is experiencing, such as pain, fatigue, fever, cough, dizziness, or shortness of breath, and attempt to translate those subjective reports into possible explanations or recommended actions.

Artificial intelligence enables this process to move beyond static, one-size-fits-all questionnaires toward more adaptive, context-aware reasoning that can respond dynamically to user input.

Early digital symptom tools relied heavily on fixed decision trees, asking the same sequence of questions regardless of context. While these systems provided basic guidance, they struggled with nuance and often failed to account for the complexity of real-world symptom presentation.

Modern AI-driven symptom checkers combine multiple computational approaches to overcome these limitations. Rule-based logic encodes established clinical knowledge, such as red-flag symptoms that require urgent attention, contraindications, and escalation thresholds. These rules act as safety guardrails, ensuring that potentially serious presentations, such as chest pain with shortness of breath or neurological deficits, are flagged promptly.

Alongside these rules, machine learning models analyze large datasets containing symptom combinations, diagnoses, demographic factors, and outcomes. By learning patterns across millions of cases, these models estimate the likelihood of different conditions and rank them according to probability or risk.

For example, a system evaluating abdominal pain may weigh symptom location, duration, associated nausea, fever, and patient age to differentiate between benign causes and conditions requiring urgent evaluation. This probabilistic reasoning allows AI systems to handle uncertainty more effectively than rigid algorithms.

Natural language processing (NLP) plays a particularly important role in symptom interpretation.

Many modern symptom checkers allow users to describe their symptoms in their own words rather than selecting from predefined lists. NLP algorithms extract relevant clinical concepts from free-text input, interpret synonyms and colloquial expressions, and normalize variations in phrasing.

For instance, "tightness in the chest," "pressure," or "a heavy feeling" may all be mapped to clinically relevant descriptors. This flexibility reduces friction for users and captures richer, more authentic information about their experience.

However, free-text input also introduces challenges. Human language is inherently ambiguous, and anxiety, cultural norms, and limited health literacy may influence symptom descriptions. So, NLP systems must distinguish between literal and figurative language, manage misspellings or incomplete sentences, and avoid overinterpreting vague descriptions.

For example, the phrase "feeling off" may indicate anything from mild fatigue to early infection. Careful model design and conservative interpretation are essential to avoid misleading recommendations.

AI-driven symptom interpretation increasingly incorporates contextual data beyond symptoms alone.

Factors such as age, sex, pregnancy status, known chronic conditions, medications, and recent medical history significantly influence risk assessment. A symptom such as shortness of breath carries very different implications in a young, healthy individual than in an older adult with heart disease. Advanced systems adjust their reasoning accordingly, weighting symptoms within the appropriate clinical context.

Some platforms also integrate data from wearables or connected devices to refine interpretation.

Elevated resting heart rate, reduced activity levels, or abnormal sleep patterns may provide additional clues about physiological stress or illness. For example, combining self-reported fever with wearable-derived heart rate trends may increase confidence in identifying an acute infection.

While such integration can improve accuracy, it also increases complexity and requires careful validation.

Importantly, AI-driven symptom checkers are not designed to deliver definitive diagnoses. Instead, they typically produce differential assessments, risk stratification, or recommendations for next steps, such as self-care, scheduling a primary care visit, or seeking urgent care. This distinction is intentional and reflects the realities of medical practice. Accurate diagnosis often requires physical examination, diagnostic testing, and clinical judgment - elements that are beyond the scope of most patient-facing digital tools. By focusing on guidance rather than diagnosis, symptom checkers aim to support timely and appropriate care-seeking behavior.

Despite technological advances, symptom interpretation remains one of the most challenging tasks for artificial intelligence. Symptoms are subjective by nature and influenced by individual perception, emotional state, cultural expectations, and communication style. Anxiety, for example, may amplify symptom reporting, while stoicism may lead others to underreport severity.

AI systems must balance sensitivity, ensuring that serious conditions are not missed, with specificity, avoiding unnecessary alarms that can drive anxiety or inappropriate healthcare utilization.

Striking this balance is central to safety and effectiveness. Overly conservative systems may recommend urgent care too frequently, burdening healthcare systems and eroding user trust.

Conversely, overly permissive systems risk under-triage and delayed care. Achieving appropriate calibration requires extensive testing, continuous monitoring, and transparent communication about limitations.

Ultimately, the use of AI for symptom interpretation represents a careful blend of clinical knowledge, data-driven inference, and human-centered design. When implemented responsibly, these systems can help individuals make more informed decisions at moments of uncertainty, serving as an entry point into the healthcare system rather than a substitute for professional care.

Decision Support Tools for Patients

AI-powered symptom checkers are best understood as decision support tools rather than diagnostic authorities. Their primary role is not to tell patients what condition they have, but to help them decide whether to seek care, what type of care is most appropriate, and how urgently action may be required.

In an increasingly fragmented and complex healthcare landscape, these tools function as navigational aids, guiding individuals through uncertainty at moments when professional care may not be immediately accessible.

For many people, the most difficult part of experiencing symptoms is determining whether they are serious enough to warrant medical attention. Minor symptoms often resolve on their own, while others may represent early signs of conditions that benefit from prompt intervention.

Symptom checkers address this uncertainty by offering structured, evidence-informed guidance that helps users weigh risk without relying solely on intuition or internet searches, which can be misleading or anxiety-provoking.

This decision support function has significant implications for healthcare utilization.

Emergency departments in many regions are overcrowded, with a substantial proportion of visits related to non-urgent conditions. At the same time, delayed care for genuinely serious symptoms can lead to worse outcomes. By encouraging self-care for low-risk situations and highlighting warning signs that require urgent attention, AI-driven symptom checkers can help balance demand across the healthcare system.

For example, a user experiencing mild upper respiratory symptoms without fever or breathing difficulty may be advised to rest and monitor symptoms at home, whereas another reporting chest pain with shortness of breath would be directed to immediate emergency evaluation.

Decision support tools typically present recommendations in the form of care pathways rather than diagnoses. These pathways may include self-care guidance, scheduling a primary care appointment, using telemedicine services, visiting an urgent care clinic, or seeking emergency care. The language used is intentionally cautious and framed around risk rather than certainty. Practical tools explain the reasoning behind recommendations, such as the presence of red-flag symptoms or risk factors, which helps build trust and supports informed decision-making.

Education is an important component of patient decision support. Many symptom checkers provide contextual information on symptom management, expected recovery timelines, and signs that warrant reassessment.

For example, a patient with musculoskeletal pain may receive guidance on rest, gentle movement, and pain relief strategies, along with clear instructions on when to seek further evaluation if symptoms worsen or fail to improve.

This educational function empowers patients to manage minor conditions safely and confidently.

AI-driven decision support can also improve continuity of care. In integrated health systems, symptom checkers may connect directly to appointment scheduling, telehealth platforms, or nurse advice lines. This integration reduces friction and makes it easier for patients to act on recommendations.

For instance, a user advised to see a clinician within 24 hours may be offered immediate options for virtual consultation or in-person appointments, lowering barriers to timely care.

From a patient experience perspective, these tools can reduce anxiety by providing structured, non-judgmental guidance. Uncertainty often drives fear, and symptom checkers that communicate calmly, transparently, and empathetically can help users feel more supported. This is particularly valuable for patients managing chronic conditions, caregivers making decisions for dependents, or people in underserved areas with limited access to healthcare professionals.

However, decision support tools must be designed and used with caution. Over-reliance on automated recommendations can delay necessary care if users misinterpret guidance or ignore escalating symptoms.

Conversely, overly conservative systems that recommend urgent care too frequently may increase healthcare utilization and erode user trust. Striking the right balance requires careful calibration, continuous monitoring, and clear communication of limitations.

Safeguards are essential. Effective symptom checkers include explicit disclaimers, encourage users to seek professional advice when uncertain, and provide easy access to human support when needed.

Rather than replacing clinician judgment, AI-driven decision support is most effective when it complements existing care pathways and empowers patients to make informed, timely decisions within a broader healthcare ecosystem.

Clinical Triage vs. Self-Assessment

A critical distinction in AI-driven triage lies between self-assessment tools and clinically integrated triage systems. Although both rely on similar underlying technologies, such as machine learning, rule-based logic, and natural language processing, their intended purposes, risk profiles, and governance requirements differ substantially.

Understanding this distinction is essential for safe deployment, appropriate use, and realistic expectations of what each type of system can and cannot do.

Self-assessment tools are designed for direct use by patients or caregivers, often outside formal healthcare settings and without real-time clinician involvement. Their primary goal is to support individuals in making preliminary decisions about whether and how to seek care.

As such, these tools prioritize accessibility, simplicity, and broad applicability across diverse populations. They are typically available via mobile apps, websites, or integrated digital health platforms. They are often used at moments of uncertainty - late at night, during travel, or when professional advice is not immediately accessible.

Because self-assessment tools operate without clinical oversight, they are generally designed to be conservative. Their algorithms err on the side of caution, especially when symptoms could plausibly indicate serious conditions. For example, a self-assessment tool may recommend urgent evaluation for chest pain even when the likelihood of a cardiac cause is low, simply to avoid the risk of under-triage.

This conservatism is a deliberate safety feature, but it can also contribute to increased healthcare utilization if not carefully calibrated.

Self-assessment tools must also accommodate wide variation in health literacy, communication style, and symptom interpretation. Users may describe symptoms imprecisely, misunderstand questions, or overestimate or underestimate severity. As a result, these systems are typically limited to providing guidance rather than definitive conclusions. Their recommendations are framed in terms of next steps, such as self-care, monitoring, or seeking professional advice, rather than diagnoses or treatment decisions.

Clinically integrated triage systems, by contrast, operate within healthcare organizations and are designed to support professional decision-making. These systems are used by nurses, call center staff, emergency department personnel, or clinicians to prioritize patients, allocate resources, and manage clinical workflows.

Because they function within regulated healthcare environments, they can access richer and more reliable data and operate under professional oversight.

AI-driven clinical triage systems often incorporate inputs beyond self-reported symptoms. These may include vital signs, medical history, laboratory results, imaging findings, medication lists, and clinician observations.

For example, in an emergency department setting, an AI triage system might analyze presenting complaints alongside heart rate, blood pressure, oxygen saturation, and past medical history to identify patients at high risk of deterioration. The system may generate priority scores, trigger escalation alerts, or recommend specific care pathways.

In outpatient or call center environments, clinical triage systems can assist nurses in managing large volumes of patient inquiries. By highlighting high-risk cases or suggesting follow-up questions, AI tools can improve consistency and efficiency while allowing clinicians to focus attention where it is most needed.

Importantly, these systems do not replace clinical judgment; rather, they augment it by synthesizing information rapidly and reducing cognitive load.

The safety expectations for clinically integrated triage systems are significantly higher than for self-assessment tools. Errors in clinical triage can have immediate and serious consequences, including delayed treatment or inappropriate resource allocation. As a result, these systems are typically subject to rigorous validation, continuous monitoring, and formal governance processes.

Performance is often evaluated against clinical benchmarks, outcomes data, and established standards of care. Regulatory oversight is also more stringent, particularly when systems influence clinical decisions or patient flow.

By contrast, self-assessment tools often fall into regulatory gray areas, particularly when positioned as informational or wellness tools rather than medical devices. While this can accelerate deployment, it also places greater responsibility on developers to design conservative, transparent systems and communicate limitations clearly to users.

Confusion between these two categories can create risk. Applying a self-assessment tool in a clinical decision-making context, such as relying on patient-facing recommendations to prioritize emergency department care, may lead to inappropriate conclusions. Conversely, exposing patients directly to outputs designed for clinical triage could cause confusion, anxiety, or misinterpretation.

Each system is optimized for its specific context and user group.

Clear boundaries are, therefore, essential. Organizations deploying AI-driven triage must define who the system is for, how it should be used, and what decisions it is authorized to inform. Training is critical, particularly for clinical staff who interact with AI recommendations. Governance frameworks should establish accountability, escalation protocols, and mechanisms for auditing performance over time.

Ultimately, both self-assessment tools and clinically integrated triage systems play important roles in modern healthcare. When used appropriately, self-assessment tools empower patients and improve access to guidance, while clinical triage systems enhance efficiency and safety within healthcare organizations.

Recognizing their differences and respecting their limitations is central to realizing the benefits of AI-driven triage without compromising patient safety or trust.

Performance Benchmarking and Safety

Ensuring the performance and safety of AI-driven symptom checkers is both essential and inherently complex.

Unlike traditional medical devices, which typically perform a single, well-defined function, symptom checkers operate in probabilistic and uncertain domains. They do not produce definitive diagnoses; instead, they generate risk assessments, ranked possibilities, or recommended next steps based on incomplete and subjective information.

As a result, evaluating their effectiveness requires a broader and more nuanced approach than conventional pass-fail testing.

Performance benchmarking for symptom checkers typically spans multiple dimensions. These include accuracy, or how closely system outputs align with accepted clinical reasoning; sensitivity, or the ability to correctly identify potentially serious conditions; specificity, or the ability to avoid unnecessary escalation; and user outcomes, such as whether recommendations lead to appropriate care-seeking behavior.

No single metric adequately captures performance, and trade-offs between these measures are unavoidable.

Benchmarking often involves comparing AI outputs against established clinical guidelines, expert clinician judgment, or real-world outcomes.

For example, evaluators may test whether a system correctly identifies red-flag symptoms such as chest pain with neurological deficits, high fever in infants, or sudden shortness of breath. Other assessments focus on whether recommended care levels, such as self-care, primary care, urgent care, or emergency services, are appropriate given the presentation. In some studies, simulated patient cases are used, while others analyze retrospective data from real users to assess downstream outcomes.

However, evaluating symptom checkers is complicated by variability in symptom presentation and user behavior. Two individuals experiencing the same condition may describe their symptoms very differently, influenced by health literacy, anxiety, cultural norms, or prior experiences. Users may also omit important details, misunderstand questions, or change responses as the interaction unfolds.

This variability makes it challenging to define a single "correct" answer and highlights the importance of testing systems across diverse populations and scenarios.

Safety considerations sit at the center of performance evaluation. One of the most significant risks is false negatives, in which a symptom checker fails to identify a serious condition or underestimates the urgency. Such errors can delay care and lead to adverse outcomes.

For example, a system that does not appropriately escalate symptoms suggestive of stroke or sepsis could have serious consequences. As a result, many symptom checkers are deliberately designed to prioritize sensitivity, even at the expense of specificity.

False positives, while generally less dangerous in the immediate sense, also carry meaningful consequences.

Overly cautious systems that recommend urgent or emergency care too frequently can increase healthcare utilization, contribute to overcrowding, and heighten user anxiety. A user repeatedly advised to seek urgent care for benign symptoms may lose trust in the tool or experience unnecessary stress. At a system level, excessive false positives can strain already limited healthcare resources.

Balancing sensitivity and specificity, therefore, requires careful calibration informed by real-world data and clinical input.

Transparency is a critical component of safety. Users must understand that symptom checkers are not diagnostic tools and that their recommendations are based on probabilities rather than certainty.

Clear explanations of why a particular recommendation is made, such as the presence of specific warning signs, can help users interpret guidance appropriately. Explicit escalation instructions, such as advising users to seek care if symptoms worsen or new symptoms develop, provide an additional safety net.

Access to human support further enhances safety. Many effective symptom checkers offer pathways to connect users with healthcare professionals, such as nurse advice lines or telemedicine services, particularly when uncertainty remains high.

This hybrid approach recognizes the limitations of automated systems and reinforces the role of human judgment in complex cases.

Regulatory oversight of symptom checkers varies widely depending on jurisdiction and intended use. Tools positioned as general informational or wellness applications may be subject to limited regulation, while systems integrated into clinical workflows or influencing medical decision-making often face stricter requirements. Regulatory bodies increasingly recognize the growing influence of symptom checkers on care navigation and are developing frameworks to address validation, accountability, and post-market surveillance.

Post-market monitoring is especially important for AI-driven systems. Unlike static software, many symptom checkers incorporate machine learning models that evolve over time as new data is incorporated.

While continuous learning can improve performance, it also introduces risk. Changes intended to enhance accuracy may inadvertently degrade performance in certain populations or scenarios. Robust governance mechanisms, including version control, audit trails, and outcome tracking, are essential to detect and address such issues promptly.

Real-world outcome monitoring is increasingly viewed as a best practice. Rather than relying solely on pre-deployment testing, organizations assess whether symptom checker recommendations lead to appropriate care-seeking behavior, timely intervention, and acceptable user experiences. Feedback loops that incorporate clinician reviews, user reports, and health system data support continuous improvement while maintaining safety.

Ultimately, performance benchmarking and safety in AI-driven symptom checkers require an ongoing, multidisciplinary effort. Technical validation, clinical oversight, regulatory engagement, and transparent communication with users must work together.

When these elements are aligned, symptom checkers can serve as reliable, supportive tools that enhance access to care without compromising safety or trust.

User Experience and Health Literacy Considerations

The effectiveness of AI-driven symptom checkers depends not only on the accuracy of their algorithms but also on how users experience and understand them.

Even the most technically advanced system will fail to deliver meaningful benefits if users cannot navigate the interface, interpret the guidance, or trust the recommendations. User experience and health literacy are therefore not secondary design considerations, but central determinants of safety, adoption, and real-world impact.

User interfaces must be intuitive, accessible, and designed for individuals who may be anxious, unwell, or under time pressure. Symptom checkers are often used at moments of uncertainty or distress, when cognitive load is high. Complex navigation, cluttered screens, or unclear instructions can quickly overwhelm users.

Effective designs prioritize simplicity, guiding users step-by-step through symptom reporting while minimizing unnecessary choices. Clear progress indicators, concise questions, and responsive layouts help maintain engagement and reduce confusion.

Language plays a critical role in user experience. Medical terminology, while precise for clinicians, can be confusing or intimidating for the general public. Terms such as "dyspnea," "palpitations," or "neurological deficit" may not be understood without explanation.

At the same time, oversimplifying language can obscure important distinctions or lead to misinterpretation. For example, describing all chest discomfort as "pain" may miss subtle but clinically relevant differences in sensation.

Successful symptom checkers strike a balance by using plain language supplemented with clarifying examples or definitions when needed.

Tone is equally important. Alarmist language can heighten anxiety and drive unnecessary healthcare utilization, while overly reassuring phrasing may downplay genuine risk. For instance, telling a user that symptoms are "probably nothing to worry about" without emphasizing monitoring or warning signs may lead to delayed care.

Conversely, frequent use of urgent language can desensitize users or erode trust over time. An empathetic, neutral tone that acknowledges uncertainty while clearly communicating risk supports more appropriate responses.

Health literacy varies widely across populations, influenced by education, cultural background, and prior healthcare experiences. Some users may struggle to accurately describe symptoms, interpret timelines, or understand conditional recommendations. AI-driven symptom checkers must therefore be designed to accommodate varying levels of health literacy.

Structured questioning, where complex concepts are broken into simpler components, can improve accuracy. Visual aids, such as body diagrams to indicate pain location or icons representing symptom severity, can help users communicate more effectively.

Adaptive explanations further enhance accessibility. Rather than presenting the same information to all users, AI systems can adjust the depth and complexity of explanations based on user responses. For example, a user who requests more detail may receive expanded guidance, while another may prefer a concise summary.

This flexibility respects individual preferences and reduces cognitive burden.

Trust is a critical determinant of whether users act on symptom checker recommendations. Users are more likely to follow guidance when they perceive the system as credible, transparent, and aligned with their interests. Trust can be reinforced by clearly explaining why certain questions are asked and how recommendations are generated.

Acknowledging uncertainty, such as stating that guidance is based on reported information and may change if symptoms evolve, helps set realistic expectations and reduces misplaced confidence.

Brand affiliation and institutional backing can also influence trust. Symptom checkers associated with recognized healthcare organizations or integrated into existing care systems may be perceived as more reliable than standalone consumer apps. However, trust can be quickly undermined by inconsistent recommendations, unexplained changes, or perceived commercial bias.

Accessibility considerations extend beyond language and literacy. Symptom checkers should accommodate users with disabilities, older adults, and individuals with limited access to technology. Features such as adjustable text size, high-contrast displays, voice input, and screen reader compatibility support users with visual or motor impairments. Mobile-first design is particularly important in regions where smartphones are the primary means of internet access. Offline or low-bandwidth functionality can further expand reach in resource-limited settings.

Ethical considerations intersect closely with user experience. Users should be clearly informed about how their data is collected, used, and protected. Consent processes should be transparent and understandable, avoiding dense legal language. Respecting autonomy means allowing users to make informed choices rather than subtly nudging them toward predetermined outcomes that may prioritize system efficiency over individual preference.

Ultimately, effective symptom checkers are not defined solely by sophisticated algorithms, but by their ability to communicate clearly, respect users, and support informed decision-making. By centering user experience and health literacy in design, AI-driven symptom checkers can become trusted tools that enhance access to care while safeguarding safety and dignity.

Conclusion

AI-driven symptom checkers and triage tools represent a powerful but nuanced application of artificial intelligence in healthcare.

By supporting early assessment, guiding care navigation, and enhancing patient decision-making, these systems address real needs in overstretched healthcare environments. When designed and deployed responsibly, they can improve access, reduce unnecessary utilization, and support timely intervention.

At the same time, symptom interpretation and triage are high-stakes activities that demand caution. Variability in symptoms, differences in user understanding, and the inherent uncertainty of early assessment require systems that prioritize safety, transparency, and human oversight. Performance benchmarking, clear boundaries between self-assessment and clinical triage, and thoughtful user experience design are essential to minimizing risk.

Symptom checkers constitute a significant component of a broader AI-enabled healthcare ecosystem. Their true value emerges when they are integrated into coordinated care pathways that combine technology, clinical expertise, and patient engagement to deliver more responsive, equitable, and human-centered care.

Chapter 5.
Early Disease Detection and Predictive Diagnostics

Early detection of diseases has long been one of the most powerful levers for improving health outcomes. Conditions identified at an early or preclinical stage are often easier to treat, less costly to manage, and associated with significantly better long-term prognosis.

Historically, early detection has relied on population screening programs, clinician vigilance, and patient-reported symptoms. While these approaches have saved countless lives, they are constrained by human capacity, variability in interpretation, and the limits of episodic care.

Artificial intelligence introduces a new paradigm for early disease detection, one that leverages large-scale data, pattern recognition, and predictive modeling to identify risk and pathology earlier, more consistently, and across broader populations. Rather than waiting for symptoms to become obvious, AI systems analyze subtle signals across imaging, biomarkers, genomics, and longitudinal health data to detect disease before it becomes clinically apparent.

This chapter examines how AI is transforming early disease detection and predictive diagnostics. It explores imaging-based detection in radiology and pathology, biomarker and genomic prediction models, early identification of chronic diseases, comparisons between AI and human interpretation, and the integration of AI into screening programs.

The focus remains on realistic clinical value, limitations, and the conditions required for safe and effective adoption.

Imaging-Based Detection (Radiology, Pathology)

Medical imaging has been one of the earliest, most mature, and most impactful domains for the application of artificial intelligence in healthcare. Radiology and pathology are inherently data-intensive specialties, generating vast volumes of visual information that must be interpreted accurately, consistently, and often under significant time pressure.

Artificial intelligence, particularly deep learning and computer vision, has proven especially well suited to these environments, where subtle visual patterns can carry critical diagnostic meaning and where human interpretation is subject to variability.

In radiology, AI systems analyze a wide range of imaging modalities, including X-rays, computed tomography (CT), magnetic resonance imaging (MRI), ultrasound, and mammography. These systems are trained on large datasets of labeled images, learning to recognize visual features associated with disease, injury, or abnormal anatomy.

Over time, deep learning models develop the ability to detect patterns that may be difficult for the human eye to perceive consistently, particularly in early-stage disease or in complex imaging studies.

Numerous applications have demonstrated clinical promise. AI algorithms have shown strong performance in detecting pulmonary nodules on chest CT scans, identifying breast lesions on mammograms, flagging intracranial hemorrhage on head CT, and recognizing fractures on X-rays.

In some cases, AI systems can identify abnormalities at earlier stages than routine visual inspection, when findings are subtle and easily overlooked. These capabilities are particularly valuable in screening contexts, where the goal is to identify disease in asymptomatic populations and where large volumes of imaging must be reviewed efficiently.

One of the most common roles of AI in radiology is as a second reader. Rather than replacing radiologists, AI systems flag areas of concern for closer inspection, helping reduce perceptual errors and oversight. In breast cancer screening, for example, AI can highlight suspicious regions that warrant further evaluation, supporting radiologists in making more informed decisions while reducing unnecessary recalls. In lung cancer screening programs, AI assists in prioritizing scans with potentially malignant nodules, enabling faster review of high-risk cases.

Consistency is a key advantage of AI in imaging-based detection. Human interpretation can vary based on training, experience, fatigue, and workload. Two radiologists may interpret the same image differently, particularly in borderline cases. AI systems, by contrast, apply the same criteria uniformly across cases, reducing variability and supporting more standardized detection. This consistency is especially valuable in high-volume environments, such as emergency departments or national screening programs, where maintaining uniform quality is challenging.

AI also contributes to efficiency. By automatically triaging imaging studies based on suspected urgency, AI systems help ensure that critical findings, such as intracranial bleeding or pneumothorax, are reviewed promptly. This prioritization does not change the final diagnostic responsibility, but it improves workflow and can reduce delays in care.

In settings with radiologist shortages, such efficiency gains are increasingly important.

In pathology, AI-driven image analysis is playing a similarly transformative role. Advances in digital pathology have enabled whole-slide imaging, converting traditional glass slides into high-resolution digital images. These slides contain enormous amounts of visual data, often far exceeding what can be comprehensively assessed by a human observer within a limited time.

AI systems can analyze entire slides at pixel-level resolution, identifying regions of interest, quantifying cellular features, and supporting classification and grading.

In oncologic pathology, AI models can assist in detecting malignant cells, estimating tumor burden, and identifying patterns associated with prognosis or treatment response.

For example, AI can quantify mitotic activity, assess tumor margins, or detect subtle morphological changes indicative of early malignancy. In inflammatory or infectious diseases, AI can support pattern recognition across large tissue areas, improving consistency and reducing diagnostic variability.

Another important contribution of AI in pathology is quantification. While human assessment is often qualitative or semi-quantitative, AI systems can provide precise measurements of features such as cell density, nuclear size, or spatial organization. These quantitative insights can support more reproducible diagnoses and enable correlations with molecular or clinical data, strengthening precision medicine approaches.

Despite these advances, AI in imaging is rarely used in isolation. The most successful and safest implementations position AI as an assistive tool rather than an autonomous decision-maker. Radiologists and pathologists remain responsible for final interpretation and clinical judgment. AI provides decision support, enhancing sensitivity, reducing oversight, and improving efficiency, while humans provide contextual understanding, ethical reasoning, and accountability.

This collaborative model is essential because imaging findings do not exist in a vacuum. Clinical history, laboratory data, patient symptoms, and prior studies all influence interpretation. AI systems, while powerful, lack the holistic understanding that clinicians bring to diagnostic reasoning.

Integrating AI outputs into existing workflows in a way that complements rather than disrupts practice is therefore critical.

Despite strong performance in controlled research settings, challenges remain in real-world deployment. Imaging datasets used to train AI models may not be representative of all populations, leading to potential bias. Differences in imaging equipment, acquisition protocols, contrast use, and image quality can affect model performance. A system trained on data from one institution may not generalize well to another without additional validation.

As a result, robust validation across diverse clinical environments is essential before widespread deployment. Continuous monitoring, recalibration, and clinician feedback are necessary to ensure ongoing reliability. Transparency about limitations and appropriate use cases helps maintain trust and prevents overreliance.

In summary, imaging-based detection in radiology and pathology represents one of the clearest demonstrations of AI's potential in healthcare. When thoughtfully integrated, AI enhances consistency, efficiency, and early detection while preserving the central role of human expertise.

Its success depends not only on technical performance, but on validation, collaboration, and responsible clinical adoption.

Biomarker and Genomic Prediction Models

Beyond medical imaging, artificial intelligence is playing an increasingly influential role in predictive diagnostics through the analysis of biomarkers and genomic data.

Biomarkers, measurable indicators of biological processes, pathogenic activity, or therapeutic response, have long been central to disease detection and monitoring. Traditionally, clinicians have relied on individual biomarker values or simple ratios interpreted against population-based reference ranges. While effective for detecting established disease, this approach is limited in its ability to capture early, subtle, or multifactorial changes.

Advances in AI now enable a more sophisticated paradigm, one that analyzes complex, multivariate, and longitudinal biomarker patterns to estimate disease risk before overt clinical manifestations appear.

Machine learning models are particularly well-suited to biomarker analysis because they can identify nonlinear relationships and interactions across multiple variables simultaneously. Rather than evaluating biomarkers in isolation, AI systems consider combinations of laboratory values, physiological signals, and molecular markers over time.

For example, early metabolic dysfunction may not be apparent from a single fasting glucose measurement, but a pattern involving mildly elevated glucose, increasing insulin levels, subtle lipid abnormalities, and changes in inflammatory markers may collectively signal rising diabetes risk.

AI models can detect such patterns long before traditional diagnostic thresholds are crossed.

This multivariate approach is especially valuable in complex conditions where no single biomarker is definitive. In cardiovascular disease, for instance, AI systems can integrate cholesterol subfractions, inflammatory markers, blood pressure trends, heart rate variability, and lifestyle data to estimate individualized risk.

Similarly, in kidney disease, subtle changes in creatinine, electrolyte balance, urine markers, and longitudinal trends may indicate early decline that would be missed by snapshot measurements alone.

By analyzing trajectories rather than static values, AI enables earlier identification and more precise risk stratification.

Longitudinal biomarker analysis also supports personalized monitoring. AI systems learn the patient's baseline physiology and detect deviations that may be clinically meaningful for that specific person, even if values remain within "normal" population ranges. This personalized baseline approach is particularly relevant for preventive care and chronic disease management, where early intervention can alter long-term outcomes.

Genomic data adds a powerful additional layer to predictive diagnostics. Advances in sequencing technologies have made it possible to generate vast datasets capturing genetic variation, gene expression, epigenetic modifications, and regulatory mechanisms. However, the sheer volume and complexity of genomic data exceed the capacity of traditional analytic methods.

AI models, particularly deep learning and ensemble approaches, can analyze these datasets to identify patterns associated with disease susceptibility, progression, and treatment response.

In oncology, AI-driven genomic prediction models are already influencing clinical practice. By analyzing tumor DNA and RNA profiles, AI systems can identify mutations associated with cancer risk, aggressiveness, and sensitivity to specific therapies.

This information supports earlier detection in high-risk individuals, more accurate prognostic assessment, and selection of targeted treatments. For example, AI models can help determine whether a tumor is likely to respond to immunotherapy or specific targeted agents based on complex genomic signatures rather than single mutations.

In cardiology, polygenic risk scores illustrate how AI transforms genomic information into actionable insight. These scores combine the effects of hundreds or thousands of genetic variants to estimate an individual's lifetime risk of cardiovascular disease. Unlike traditional risk factors, which often become apparent later in life, genetic risk is present from birth. AI-driven risk stratification enables earlier preventive strategies, such as intensified lifestyle modification or closer monitoring, long before disease develops.

Genomic prediction models also play a role in inherited disorders and rare diseases, where AI can assist in identifying pathogenic variants among vast numbers of benign genetic differences. By prioritizing likely disease-causing mutations, AI supports faster diagnosis and reduces the diagnostic odyssey that many patients with rare conditions experience.

However, in spite of their promise, biomarker and genomic prediction models introduce important challenges that must be addressed carefully.

One key limitation is that genetic or biomarker-based risk does not equate to certainty. Most common diseases arise from complex interactions between genetics, environment, lifestyle, and social determinants of health. A high genetic risk score does not guarantee disease, just as a low-risk score does not confer immunity.

Overinterpretation of predictive results can lead to unnecessary anxiety, stigmatization, or overtreatment.

Communication is therefore critical. AI-generated risk estimates must be presented in a way that emphasizes probability rather than inevitability and clearly explains modifiable versus non-modifiable factors.

For example, patients with elevated genetic risk for cardiovascular disease may benefit from targeted prevention, but they should also understand that lifestyle choices can substantially modify actual outcomes.

Another challenge lies in data representation and bias. Genomic datasets used to train AI models have historically underrepresented certain populations, limiting generalizability. Biomarker reference patterns may also differ across ethnic, age, and sex groups.

Without careful validation and inclusive data, predictive models risk perpetuating health disparities.

Ethical considerations further complicate genomic prediction. Questions around consent, data ownership, and secondary use of genetic information are particularly sensitive. Unlike many other health data types, genomic information has implications not only for patients but also for their family members. Robust governance frameworks and clear patient education are, hence, essential to ensure responsible use.

In summary, biomarker and genomic prediction models represent a major advance in early disease detection and preventive medicine. By moving beyond single measurements toward integrated, longitudinal, and personalized analysis, AI enables earlier risk identification and more tailored intervention strategies.

However, realizing this potential requires careful calibration, transparent communication, and ethical deployment. When integrated thoughtfully into clinical care, AI-driven biomarker and genomic models shift diagnostics from reactive identification to proactive risk management - an essential step toward truly personalized healthcare.

Early Identification of Chronic Diseases

Chronic diseases, such as diabetes, cardiovascular disease, chronic kidney disease, and neurodegenerative disorders, represent some of the greatest challenges facing modern healthcare systems. These conditions typically develop slowly and silently, often over many years, before becoming clinically apparent. By the time symptoms prompt medical attention, substantial physiological damage may already have occurred, limiting treatment options and increasing long-term costs.

Artificial intelligence offers powerful tools to address this gap by enabling earlier identification of chronic disease risk and progression through the analysis of longitudinal health data.

Traditional healthcare models rely heavily on episodic measurements collected during clinic visits. While valuable, these snapshots provide limited insight into how health evolves over time.

In contrast, electronic health records, wearable devices, and remote monitoring systems generate continuous streams of real-world data that reflect daily behaviors, physiological responses, and environmental influences. AI models are uniquely suited to analyzing these complex, longitudinal datasets, identifying subtle trends and patterns that may signal early disease development long before diagnostic thresholds are crossed.

In metabolic diseases, such as type 2 diabetes, AI systems can integrate data on body weight, physical activity, sleep patterns, laboratory values, and medication history to estimate individual risk.

For example, gradual increases in fasting glucose combined with declining activity levels and disrupted sleep may collectively indicate rising insulin resistance. Identifying these patterns early enables targeted lifestyle interventions, such as dietary modification, increased physical activity, or weight management, that can delay or even prevent disease onset.

Such preventive strategies are often far more effective and less costly than treating established disease.

Cardiovascular disease provides another illustrative example. AI-driven predictive models analyze blood pressure trends, lipid profiles, inflammatory markers, heart rate variability, and behavioral data to estimate long-term risk of events such as heart attack or stroke. These models can identify high-risk patients years before symptoms appear, supporting earlier initiation of preventive measures.

By personalizing risk assessment, AI enables more precise allocation of interventions, such as intensified lifestyle counseling or closer clinical monitoring, rather than applying uniform strategies across entire populations.

Chronic kidney disease also benefits from early AI-driven detection. Subtle declines in kidney function, changes in electrolyte balance, or rising protein levels in urine may progress gradually and go unnoticed in routine care. AI systems can analyze longitudinal laboratory trends to identify early decline and alert clinicians to intervene before irreversible damage occurs.

Early management can slow progression, reduce complications, and improve quality of life.

In neurodegenerative diseases, early identification remains particularly challenging due to the absence of definitive early biomarkers. AI-driven analysis offers new possibilities by examining nontraditional data sources. Changes in speech patterns, gait, fine motor control, or performance on cognitive tasks may precede clinical diagnosis of conditions such as Parkinson’s or Alzheimer’s disease.

For example, subtle alterations in voice modulation or typing behavior have been explored as early indicators of neurological change. While many of these applications remain under active research and are not yet widely deployed, they illustrate the potential of AI to extend detection into preclinical stages where interventions may be more effective.

Early identification of chronic disease also supports more efficient healthcare delivery at the system level. By stratifying populations according to risk, health systems can focus resources on individuals most likely to benefit from intervention. High-risk patients may receive more intensive monitoring, education, or support, while lower-risk individuals continue with routine care. This targeted approach improves outcomes while helping control costs and reduce unnecessary utilization.

However, early identification must be implemented responsibly. Predictive insights should be communicated clearly, emphasizing risk rather than certainty and highlighting actionable steps. Overdiagnosis or excessive monitoring can cause anxiety and strain resources if not carefully managed.

In summary, AI-driven early identification of chronic diseases represents a shift from reactive treatment to proactive prevention. By uncovering subtle patterns in longitudinal data, AI enables earlier intervention, more personalized care, and more sustainable healthcare systems.

AI Accuracy vs. Human Interpretation

A central and often debated question in AI-driven diagnostics is how the accuracy of artificial intelligence compares with human interpretation.

In many narrowly defined tasks, AI systems have demonstrated performance that is comparable to, and in some cases exceeds, that of experienced clinicians. This has generated significant optimism about AI's potential to improve diagnostic accuracy and efficiency, while also raising concerns about overreliance, loss of professional autonomy, and the appropriate role of human judgment in clinical decision-making.

AI systems excel in tasks that involve pattern recognition across large datasets.

In imaging-based diagnostics, for example, deep learning models can analyze thousands of images rapidly and consistently, identifying subtle visual features that may be difficult for the human eye to detect reliably.

Studies have shown AI performing at an expert level in tasks such as detecting diabetic retinopathy from retinal images, identifying lung nodules on CT scans, or flagging fractures on X-rays. In these contexts, AI's strengths lie in its ability to process large volumes of data without fatigue and to apply the same criteria uniformly across cases.

However, accuracy in controlled evaluations does not tell the whole story. Human clinicians bring capabilities that AI systems do not possess. Clinical interpretation extends beyond pattern recognition to include contextual understanding, ethical reasoning, and integration of nuanced information that may not be captured in structured data.

A clinician considers a patient's history, preferences, social circumstances, and evolving clinical picture when making decisions. They also manage uncertainty, communicate risk, and adapt recommendations based on individual values and goals. These functions remain outside the scope of current AI systems.

Importantly, AI and human interpretation are not competing forces, but complementary ones. AI systems may identify patterns or anomalies that humans overlook, particularly in high-volume or high-pressure environments where cognitive load is high. Clinicians, in turn, evaluate AI outputs, assess their relevance, and determine how they should influence care.

For example, an AI algorithm may flag a suspicious lesion on a mammogram, but the radiologist considers prior imaging, patient history, and overall risk before determining the appropriate next step.

Studies comparing AI and human performance often focus on specific tasks under controlled conditions, such as image classification or risk prediction using curated datasets. While these studies are useful for benchmarking, real-world diagnostic accuracy depends on many additional factors.

Workflow integration, data quality, user interface design, and clinician trust all influence whether AI improves or hinders performance. A highly accurate model that disrupts workflow or generates excessive false alarms may reduce overall effectiveness in practice.

Hybrid models that combine AI and human expertise consistently outperform either alone.

In radiology, for example, AI-assisted reading has been shown to improve detection rates while reducing oversight. In pathology, AI can pre-screen slides and highlight regions of interest, allowing pathologists to focus attention where it is most needed. In clinical decision support, predictive models can surface risk information that clinicians incorporate into broader clinical reasoning.

Understanding limitations is essential for responsible adoption. AI systems are constrained by the data on which they are trained and may perform poorly when applied to populations or settings that differ from those data. Humans are essential for recognizing when AI outputs may be unreliable or inappropriate.

Moreover, accountability in healthcare remains firmly human-centered; clinicians are responsible for decisions and outcomes, regardless of whether AI tools are involved.

Ultimately, the question is not whether AI is more accurate than humans, but how AI can be used to enhance human performance. When deployed as a decision-support tool rather than a replacement,

AI can improve consistency, reduce cognitive burden, and extend diagnostic capacity.

Responsible integration depends on recognizing the complementary strengths of AI and clinicians and designing systems that support collaboration rather than substitution.

Integration into Screening Programs

The integration of artificial intelligence into population-based screening programs represents one of the most impactful and scalable applications of early disease detection.

Screening programs are designed to identify disease in asymptomatic patients, often before clinical signs emerge, with the goal of improving outcomes through earlier intervention. While these programs have saved countless lives, they also face persistent challenges related to cost, false positives, overdiagnosis, and limited workforce capacity.

AI offers tools to address many of these challenges while enhancing the overall effectiveness of screening initiatives.

One of the primary contributions of AI to screening programs is improved efficiency. Screening generates large volumes of data, particularly in imaging-based programs such as mammography, lung cancer screening, and colorectal imaging. Radiologists and clinicians must review thousands of normal or low-risk cases to identify relatively few abnormalities.

AI systems can assist by analyzing images rapidly and consistently, flagging suspicious findings for closer review. In breast cancer screening, for example, AI algorithms have demonstrated the ability to identify lesions that warrant further evaluation while reducing unnecessary recalls, which can cause anxiety and increase costs.

In lung cancer screening, AI helps manage the complexity of interpreting low-dose CT scans, where benign nodules are common and distinguishing clinically significant findings can be challenging. By assessing features such as size, shape, and growth patterns over time, AI systems support more consistent interpretation and help prioritize cases that require prompt follow-up.

This triage function is particularly valuable in high-volume screening programs with limited specialist availability.

Beyond efficiency, AI enables more personalized screening strategies through risk stratification. Traditional screening programs often apply uniform criteria and intervals based on age or sex alone. AI-driven models integrate a broader range of factors, including family history, genetic risk, lifestyle behaviors, and prior screening results, to estimate individual risk more accurately.

This approach allows health systems to tailor screening frequency and modality to those most likely to benefit, while reducing unnecessary screening in low-risk individuals.

Personalized screening has the potential to improve outcomes while minimizing harm. Over-screening can lead to false positives, unnecessary procedures, and psychological distress. Under-screening, conversely, may miss opportunities for early detection.

AI-driven risk assessment helps balance these trade-offs by aligning screening intensity with individual risk profiles.

Successful integration of AI into screening programs requires careful evaluation and governance. Screening decisions affect large populations, and errors can have widespread consequences. AI systems must be rigorously validated across diverse populations and clinical settings to ensure consistent performance. Regulatory oversight is also essential to establish accountability, define acceptable use, and monitor ongoing performance after deployment.

Public trust is equally critical. Screening programs rely on broad participation to be effective, and skepticism about AI could undermine uptake. Transparency about how AI is used, what its limitations are, and how decisions are made helps build confidence.

Clear communication ensures that individuals understand AI's role as a support tool rather than an autonomous decision-maker.

In summary, AI has the potential to transform screening programs by improving efficiency, enabling personalized strategies, and supporting earlier detection at scale. When integrated responsibly, with rigorous validation and transparent governance, AI-enhanced screening can strengthen public health efforts while preserving safety, equity, and trust.

Conclusion

Early disease detection and predictive diagnostics represent one of the most promising applications of artificial intelligence in healthcare.

By analyzing imaging data, biomarkers, genomics, and longitudinal health records, AI systems enable earlier identification of disease, more precise risk stratification, and more effective prevention strategies.

At the same time, AI is not a substitute for clinical judgment. Its value lies in augmenting human expertise, improving consistency, and extending detection beyond the limits of episodic care. Responsible integration into clinical practice and screening programs requires rigorous validation, ethical governance, and thoughtful collaboration between technology and medicine.

As healthcare continues to shift toward prevention and personalization, AI-driven early detection will play an increasingly central role, provided it is implemented with realism, transparency, and a clear focus on patient benefit.

Chapter 6. Robotic and Image-Guided Surgeries

Surgery has always been at the forefront of medical innovation. From the introduction of anesthesia and antisepsis to minimally invasive techniques and advanced imaging, each technological shift has aimed to improve precision, safety, and patient outcomes.

Artificial intelligence now represents the next major evolution in surgical care. When combined with robotic platforms and image-guided systems, AI is transforming how surgeries are planned, performed, and evaluated.

Robotic and image-guided surgeries do not replace surgeons. Rather, they extend human capability. These systems enhance visualization, reduce physical limitations, and enable data-driven decision-making before, during, and after procedures. AI enables the analysis of vast amounts of anatomical, procedural, and outcome data, providing surgeons with real-time insights previously inaccessible.

This chapter explores the role of AI in robotic and image-guided surgery, beginning with the types of surgical robotics currently in use. It also examines AI's contributions to preoperative planning, real-time intraoperative assistance, postoperative outcome prediction, and the training of surgeons for AI-assisted procedures.

The emphasis remains on patient safety, clinical value, and the responsible integration of technology into surgical practice.

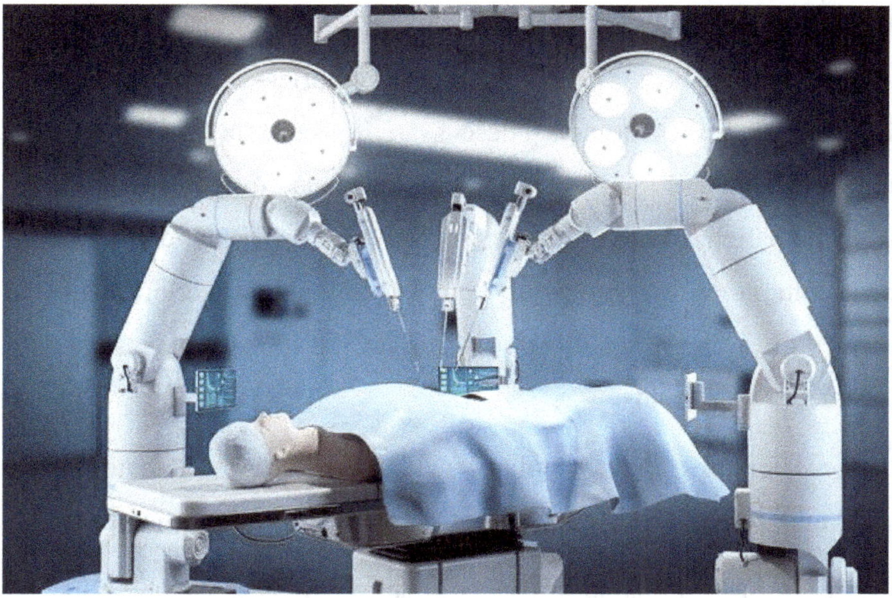

Types of Surgical Robotics

Surgical robotics encompasses a diverse set of technologies designed to enhance the surgeon's capabilities by improving precision, visualization, and control during operative procedures. Rather than replacing surgeons, these systems act as sophisticated extensions of human skill, enabling more refined movements, better access to complex anatomy, and improved ergonomics.

While surgical robots vary widely in complexity and application, most systems currently in clinical use function as surgeon-controlled, computer-assisted tools rather than autonomous operators.

This distinction is critical to understanding both their capabilities and their limitations.

One of the most widely adopted categories is robot-assisted minimally invasive surgery. These systems translate the surgeon's hand movements at a console into highly precise instrument actions within the patient's body. Robotic arms offer a greater range of motion than the human wrist, along with tremor filtration and motion scaling, which allows large hand movements to be translated into fine instrument adjustments.

These features are particularly valuable in confined anatomical spaces and during delicate maneuvers such as suturing or dissection.

Robot-assisted minimally invasive systems have been widely adopted in urology, gynecology, general surgery, and cardiothoracic surgery.

In prostate cancer surgery, for example, robotic platforms enable precise dissection around nerves responsible for continence and sexual function. In gynecologic procedures, robotics supports complex hysterectomies and endometriosis surgery with improved visualization and reduced surgeon fatigue. For patients, these approaches often result in smaller incisions, less blood loss, reduced postoperative pain, and faster recovery compared to open surgery.

Another important category is image-guided robotic systems, which integrate imaging data with robotic assistance to enhance spatial accuracy. These systems are commonly used in orthopedic surgery, neurosurgery, and spinal procedures, where millimeter-level precision is essential.

Preoperative imaging, such as CT or MRI, is used to create three-dimensional anatomical models, which guide surgical planning and instrument placement. During surgery, the robotic system helps align instruments or implants according to the preoperative plan while allowing the surgeon to retain full decision-making authority.

In orthopedic joint replacement, for instance, image-guided robotics assists in implant positioning and alignment based on the patient's unique anatomy. Accurate alignment is critical for joint function and implant longevity, and AI-enhanced planning tools can optimize placement to improve outcomes.

In spinal surgery, robotic guidance supports precise screw placement, reducing the risk of nerve injury and improving consistency across cases. In neurosurgery, robotic systems assist with stereotactic procedures, enabling accurate targeting of deep brain structures while minimizing damage to surrounding tissue.

A third category includes robotic endoscopy and catheter-based systems, which facilitate navigation through narrow, tortuous, or hard-to-reach anatomical pathways. These systems are used in interventional cardiology, pulmonology, gastroenterology, and vascular procedures.

Robotic catheters and endoscopes provide enhanced steerability and stability, allowing clinicians to reach areas that may be difficult or impossible to access manually.

AI-enhanced navigation algorithms play a key role in these systems.

By integrating imaging data and real-time feedback, AI helps map anatomical pathways, avoid critical structures, and suggest optimal routes. In robotic bronchoscopy, for example, AI-guided navigation enables more accurate targeting of small lung nodules for biopsy, improving diagnostic yield while reducing complications. In interventional cardiology, robotic catheter systems improve precision and minimize radiation exposure to clinicians.

While fully autonomous surgical robots remain largely experimental and confined to research settings, partial automation is becoming increasingly common.

Examples include automated camera control that tracks surgical instruments, robotic assistance with suturing or knot tying, and motion scaling that enhances fine motor control. These features are enabled by AI models trained on large datasets of surgical motions and outcomes.

Importantly, autonomy is tightly constrained, with safety mechanisms that allow surgeons to intervene or override the system at any time.

The adoption of surgical robotics depends on more than technical capability alone. Cost is a significant consideration, as robotic systems require substantial investment in equipment, maintenance, and consumables.

Training is also equally critical. Surgeons and operating room staff must develop new skills to use robotic platforms effectively and safely. Workflow integration is another challenge, as robotic procedures may initially increase setup time and require adjustments to operating room processes.

Finally, evidence of improved outcomes is essential to justify widespread adoption. While many robotic procedures offer clear ergonomic and technical advantages, ongoing research continues to evaluate their impact on patient outcomes, cost-effectiveness, and long-term value.

As AI becomes more deeply embedded in surgical robotics, transparency, validation, and governance become increasingly essential to maintain trust among clinicians and patients alike.

So, surgical robotics encompasses a spectrum of technologies that enhance surgical precision and control across multiple specialties. When combined with artificial intelligence and integrated thoughtfully into clinical practice, these systems have the potential to improve outcomes while preserving the central role of the surgeon in decision-making and patient care.

AI in Preoperative Planning

Preoperative planning is one of the most critical determinants of surgical success. Decisions made before a patient enters the operating room, such as the surgical approach, access points, instrument selection, sequencing of steps, and risk mitigation strategies, shape not only intraoperative performance but also postoperative recovery and long-term outcomes.

Traditionally, preoperative planning has relied on surgeons' experience, review of two-dimensional imaging, and standardized protocols. Artificial intelligence has significantly expanded this process by enabling more detailed, personalized, and predictive planning that accounts for individual anatomy, risk profiles, and procedural complexity.

AI-driven preoperative planning typically begins with advanced medical image analysis. Machine learning and computer vision algorithms process imaging data from CT scans, MRI, ultrasound, and other modalities to generate high-resolution, three-dimensional reconstructions of patient anatomy.

These models provide surgeons with a more intuitive and comprehensive understanding of spatial relationships, allowing them to visualize structures from multiple angles and anticipate potential challenges. AI systems can automatically segment organs, tumors, blood vessels, nerves, and bone structures. These tasks are time-consuming and prone to variability when performed manually.

In complex oncologic surgeries, for example, AI-assisted visualization can delineate tumor margins with greater precision and highlight proximity to critical structures such as major blood vessels or nerves. Surgeons can simulate different resection strategies and evaluate how changes in approach may affect margins, functional preservation, and complication risk.

Similarly, in orthopedic reconstruction, AI-generated anatomical models help surgeons understand variations in bone geometry, joint alignment, and load distribution that may influence implant selection and positioning.

Preoperative planning becomes even more powerful when integrated with robotic surgical systems.

In robotic surgery, planning software often connects directly to the robotic platform, translating anatomical models into actionable guidance. AI algorithms can recommend optimal port placement, instrument trajectories, and camera angles based on patient-specific anatomy and prior procedural data.

This level of precision is particularly important in minimally invasive surgery, where limited access and restricted visualization magnify the impact of small errors. Poor port placement can compromise reach, increase operative time, or raise the risk of complications. But AI-assisted planning can help mitigate these risks before surgery begins.

AI-driven planning also supports procedural simulation. Surgeons can rehearse operations in a virtual environment, testing different strategies and anticipating potential complications. For example, in liver surgery, AI models can simulate how different resection paths affect remaining liver volume and blood flow, supporting safer decision-making.

In spine surgery, AI-assisted planning allows surgeons to visualize screw trajectories and alignment before entering the operating room, reducing the likelihood of intraoperative adjustments.

Another critical application of AI in preoperative planning is risk stratification. By analyzing large datasets that include patient demographics, comorbidities, imaging findings, laboratory values, and historical surgical outcomes, AI models can estimate the likelihood of complications such as bleeding, infection, thromboembolic events, or prolonged recovery.

These predictions help surgeons and care teams tailor perioperative strategies, such as selecting minimally invasive approaches, optimizing anesthesia plans, or planning enhanced postoperative monitoring.

Risk stratification also supports more informed consent discussions. Rather than relying on population-level statistics, surgeons can discuss individualized risk profiles with patients, improving transparency and shared decision-making.

For example, a patient with multiple comorbidities undergoing abdominal surgery may benefit from prehabilitation or alternative treatment strategies identified through AI-driven risk assessment.

Personalization is a defining strength of AI-enhanced preoperative planning. Traditional surgical protocols often rely on standardized approaches that may not account fully for individual anatomical or biomechanical differences.

AI allows surgeons to adapt strategies to the patient rather than fitting the patient to the procedure. In joint replacement surgery, for instance, AI can assist in selecting implant size, alignment, and positioning optimized for the patient's unique biomechanics, potentially improving function and implant longevity.

In cardiac surgery, AI-assisted planning can help tailor graft selection and placement based on vascular anatomy and disease distribution.

Despite these advances, AI-driven preoperative planning does not eliminate uncertainty.

The accuracy of AI recommendations depends heavily on data quality, imaging resolution, and the assumptions embedded within models. Incomplete imaging, anatomical anomalies, or unexpected intraoperative findings can limit the usefulness of preoperative plans.

Moreover, AI systems are trained on historical data, which may not fully capture rare presentations or novel surgical techniques.

For these reasons, AI should be viewed as an enhancement to, rather than a replacement for, surgical judgment. Surgeons must critically evaluate AI-generated insights, understand their limitations, and integrate them with clinical experience and real-time assessment.

The most effective use of AI in preoperative planning occurs when it supports preparation, anticipation, and decision-making while preserving flexibility and human oversight.

In short, AI has transformed preoperative planning by enabling more detailed anatomical visualization, personalized strategy development, and predictive risk assessment. When integrated thoughtfully into surgical workflows, AI supports safer, more precise, and more patient-centered care, thus laying the groundwork for improved intraoperative performance and postoperative outcomes.

Real-Time Assistance and Precision Interventions

The intraoperative phase is where AI-assisted robotic and image-guided systems demonstrate their most immediate and visible impact on surgical practice.

During surgery, decisions must be made rapidly, often under conditions of limited visibility, physical constraint, and high cognitive load. Artificial intelligence supports surgeons in this environment by enhancing precision, situational awareness, and real-time decision-making while preserving human control and accountability.

One of the most significant contributions of AI during surgery is enhanced visualization.

Computer vision algorithms analyze live video feeds from laparoscopic, endoscopic, or robotic cameras to understand what the surgeon is seeing in real time. These systems can identify anatomical landmarks, differentiate tissue types, and highlight critical structures such as blood vessels, nerves, or ducts that may be difficult to distinguish visually.

In minimally invasive procedures, where depth perception and tactile feedback are reduced, this augmented visualization helps surgeons maintain orientation and spatial awareness.

For example, during laparoscopic gallbladder surgery, AI systems can highlight the biliary anatomy to reduce the risk of bile duct injury, which is a known and serious complication. In colorectal surgery, AI-assisted visualization can help delineate tumor margins or identify vascular structures that must be preserved.

These overlays do not replace the surgeon's view but provide contextual cues that support safer navigation through complex anatomy.

Instrument tracking is closely related to enhanced visualization. AI systems continuously monitor the position and movement of surgical instruments relative to anatomical structures. This capability enables real-time feedback on instrument proximity to critical areas and supports more precise control.

In robotic surgery, where movements are mediated through computer interfaces, AI-driven tracking improves alignment between intent and execution.

Another major area of impact is motion assistance. Robotic platforms equipped with AI algorithms can stabilize instruments, filter out physiologic tremor, and apply motion scaling so that large hand movements translate into fine, controlled instrument actions.

These features are particularly valuable during microsurgical tasks such as suturing, vessel anastomosis, or dissection near delicate structures.

AI-enabled motion constraints, often referred to as “virtual boundaries” or “no-go zones,” represent a significant safety enhancement. In neurosurgery, for example, AI systems can identify regions associated with a high risk of neurological damage based on preoperative imaging and intraoperative updates. If an instrument approaches these regions, the system may resist further movement or alert the surgeon.

Importantly, these constraints are assistive rather than prohibitive. They allow surgeons to retain the ability to override them when clinically necessary.

AI also supports real-time decision-making by monitoring procedural progress and comparing it to expected patterns derived from large datasets of prior surgeries. By learning what typical procedural sequences and tissue responses look like, AI systems can recognize deviations that may signal emerging risk.

For instance, unusual bleeding patterns, prolonged tissue manipulation, or deviations from planned surgical steps may trigger alerts. These alerts are designed to be supportive rather than disruptive.

Effective systems prioritize relevance and minimize unnecessary interruptions, recognizing that excessive or poorly timed alerts can increase cognitive burden rather than reduce it. For example, instead of issuing constant notifications, AI systems may escalate alerts only when multiple risk indicators converge, such as increasing blood loss combined with prolonged operative time.

In image-guided interventions, AI plays a critical role in maintaining accuracy as anatomy changes during surgery.

Preoperative imaging provides a detailed map of anatomy, but tissues may shift due to patient positioning, surgical manipulation, or physiological changes. AI systems continuously update anatomical models using intraoperative imaging modalities such as ultrasound, fluoroscopy, or intraoperative CT.

By reconciling preoperative plans with real-time data, AI maintains alignment between the surgical plan and the actual operative field.

This capability is particularly valuable in tumor resections, where removing tissue alters anatomy progressively. AI-assisted image guidance helps surgeons track remaining tumor boundaries and avoid critical structures as conditions evolve. In spinal surgery, AI can account for changes in alignment during correction procedures, supporting precise placement of instrumentation despite intraoperative shifts.

Precision interventions enabled by AI also contribute to consistency across cases and operators. Surgical outcomes can vary based on experience, fatigue, and individual technique. AI-assisted guidance helps standardize certain aspects of performance, reducing variability while still allowing surgeons to adapt to patient-specific factors.

This consistency is especially important in high-volume environments or training settings, where maintaining uniform quality can be challenging.

However, real-time AI assistance must be implemented carefully. Excessive guidance, rigid constraints, or poorly designed alerts can interfere with surgical flow and reduce trust in the system. Surgeons must be able to customize assistance levels, control when and how AI input is presented, and understand the rationale behind recommendations.

Transparency and user-centered design are essential to ensure that AI supports rather than distracts.

It is also important to recognize that AI systems are dependent on data quality and system calibration. Poor imaging, occluded views, or atypical anatomy can limit the reliability of real-time analysis.

Surgeons must remain vigilant and prepared to rely solely on their expertise when AI inputs are uncertain or unavailable.

So, real-time assistance and precision interventions represent one of the most powerful applications of AI in surgery. By enhancing visualization, stabilizing motion, supporting decision-making, and adapting to dynamic anatomy, AI-assisted systems extend human capability while preserving surgeon control.

When designed and deployed thoughtfully, these tools improve precision, safety, and consistency, thus transforming the intraoperative environment into a collaborative space where technology and human expertise work in concert.

Postoperative Outcome Predictions

Artificial intelligence's role in robotic and image-guided surgery does not end when the procedure is completed.

Postoperative outcome prediction has emerged as a powerful application of AI, supporting recovery planning, complication prevention, and continuous improvement in surgical quality. By extending analysis beyond the operating room, AI helps clinicians anticipate challenges, personalize follow-up care, and improve both patient experience and system efficiency.

Machine learning models used for outcome prediction integrate a wide range of data sources. These include patient characteristics such as age, comorbidities, functional status, and social factors, as well as intraoperative data like operative time, blood loss, instrument trajectories, tissue handling metrics, and adherence to surgical plans.

Historical outcome data from similar procedures further enrich these models, enabling them to identify patterns associated with favorable or adverse postoperative trajectories.

One of the most critical uses of postoperative outcome prediction is risk stratification. AI systems can estimate the likelihood of complications such as surgical site infection, readmission, delayed wound healing, thromboembolic events, or postoperative functional impairment. By identifying patients at higher risk early, care teams can tailor postoperative management accordingly.

For example, a patient at higher risk of infection may benefit from closer wound monitoring, extended antibiotic prophylaxis, or earlier follow-up visits.

In orthopedic surgery, AI-driven outcome prediction models are increasingly used to forecast recovery trajectories following procedures such as joint replacement or spinal surgery. By analyzing factors like implant alignment, surgical precision, rehabilitation adherence, and baseline mobility, AI systems can estimate expected recovery timelines and functional outcomes.

Patients predicted to experience slower recovery may be referred proactively to physical therapy, receive additional support for pain management, or be enrolled in remote monitoring programs to track progress at home.

Remote monitoring represents another area where outcome prediction and postoperative care intersect.

AI systems can flag deviations from expected recovery patterns based on wearable data, patient-reported outcomes, or follow-up imaging. For instance, reduced activity levels, abnormal vital signs, or worsening pain scores may prompt early intervention before complications become severe. This proactive approach shifts postoperative care from reactive management to continuous oversight.

Postoperative outcome prediction also plays a role in quality improvement and value-based care.

By aggregating predictions and outcomes across patient populations, health systems can identify factors associated with better or worse results. These insights support refinement of surgical protocols, optimization of perioperative pathways, and more effective resource allocation.

For example, if AI analysis reveals that certain preoperative factors strongly predict prolonged recovery, health systems may invest in prehabilitation programs to address those risks proactively.

Importantly, the ethical use of outcome prediction models requires careful consideration.

Predictions should be used to inform care planning, not to deny access to surgery or bias decision-making against certain patients. Risk estimates must be presented as probabilities rather than certainties, and clinicians should contextualize predictions within the broader clinical picture.

Transparency about model limitations, data sources, and uncertainty is essential, particularly when predictions influence patient expectations or shared decision-making.

Patients should also be engaged in how predictions are used. Clear communication helps ensure that predictive insights empower patients rather than increase anxiety. For example, framing a higher-risk prediction as an opportunity for enhanced support and monitoring reinforces a collaborative approach to recovery.

In short, postoperative outcome predictions extend the benefits of AI-assisted surgery beyond the operating room. By anticipating complications, personalizing recovery pathways, and supporting quality improvement, AI enables more proactive, patient-centered surgical care when its use remains transparent, ethical, and firmly grounded in clinical judgment.

Training Surgeons for AI-Assisted Procedures

The integration of artificial intelligence and robotic systems into surgical practice has profound implications for surgical training and workforce development. As operating rooms become increasingly digital and data-driven, surgeons must acquire competencies that extend beyond traditional technical skills.

In addition to anatomical knowledge and manual dexterity, modern surgeons are expected to understand system behavior, interpret AI-generated insights, and collaborate effectively with intelligent tools while maintaining full responsibility for clinical decision-making.

One of the most significant shifts in training is the growing role of simulation-based education.

AI-driven surgical simulators can replicate complex procedures with high fidelity, allowing trainees to practice in realistic, risk-free environments. These simulators incorporate anatomical variability, procedural complexity, and unexpected complications, helping trainees develop technical proficiency and situational awareness before operating on patients.

Unlike traditional simulation, AI-enhanced platforms provide objective, data-driven feedback by analyzing motion efficiency, instrument handling, precision, and error rates.

For example, in robotic-assisted surgery training, simulators can track instrument trajectories, tremor control, and task completion times, offering personalized feedback tailored to each trainee's performance. AI systems can identify recurring inefficiencies or unsafe maneuvers and suggest targeted exercises to address specific weaknesses.

This individualized approach accelerates skill acquisition and supports more consistent competency development across trainees.

AI also enables continuous skill assessment throughout a surgeon's career. Traditional metrics such as case volume or subjective evaluations provide limited insight into technical performance. In contrast, AI-driven assessment tools analyze objective data collected during real or simulated procedures, offering a more granular and reproducible evaluation of proficiency.

These tools can help training programs determine readiness for independent practice and identify areas where additional supervision or training is needed.

Experienced surgeons also benefit from continuous feedback. As new techniques, technologies, and AI-assisted systems are introduced, even highly skilled clinicians must adapt. AI-driven analytics support lifelong learning by highlighting opportunities for refinement, efficiency improvement, or adoption of best practices observed across large datasets of surgical cases.

Crucially, training must address not only how to use AI-assisted systems, but also how to critically evaluate and override them when necessary. Also, AI systems are not infallible. They are influenced by data quality, model assumptions, and contextual limitations. Surgeons must understand potential failure modes, recognize when AI recommendations may be unreliable, and maintain the confidence to rely on clinical judgment in unexpected situations.

This emphasis reinforces the surgeon's role as the ultimate decision-maker and safeguards patient safety.

Ethical and professional considerations are also central to training. Surgeons must learn how to communicate the role of AI to patients, explain its benefits and limitations, and address concerns related to trust and transparency. Training programs should incorporate discussions of accountability, consent, and data governance to ensure responsible use of AI technologies.

Cultural adaptation within surgical teams is equally important. Successful adoption of AI-assisted procedures depends on trust, shared understanding, and alignment with professional values. Training environments should emphasize that AI is a tool designed to enhance surgical care, reduce variability, and support excellence, and not a replacement for human expertise or professional autonomy.

This means training surgeons for AI-assisted procedures requires a comprehensive approach that combines technical skill development, system literacy, ethical awareness, and cultural integration.

By preparing surgeons to collaborate effectively with intelligent systems while preserving human judgment, healthcare organizations can ensure that AI enhances surgical practice in a safe, ethical, and patient-centered manner.

Conclusion

Robotic and image-guided surgeries represent one of the most sophisticated and impactful applications of artificial intelligence in healthcare. By enhancing preoperative planning, real-time precision, postoperative outcome prediction, and surgical training, AI-enabled systems extend human capability while preserving the central role of the surgeon.

However, these technologies demand rigorous validation, thoughtful integration, and continuous oversight. Their success depends not only on technical performance but also on training, governance, and ethical deployment. When implemented responsibly, AI-assisted robotic surgery has the potential to improve outcomes, reduce variability, and redefine the future of surgical care - one where precision, personalization, and human expertise work in concert rather than in competition.

Chapter 7: Disease Monitoring and Progression Tracking

Disease monitoring has traditionally been episodic. Patients are assessed during clinic visits, hospital admissions, or scheduled follow-ups, and clinical decisions are based on snapshots of health taken weeks or months apart.

While this approach has been the foundation of modern medicine, it is poorly aligned with the reality of chronic and progressive disease. Conditions such as diabetes, heart failure, asthma, autoimmune disorders, neurodegenerative disease, and cancer evolve continuously, not in discrete clinical encounters.

Artificial intelligence fundamentally reshapes this paradigm. By enabling continuous data collection, real-time analysis, and longitudinal pattern recognition, AI allows healthcare systems to move from reactive disease management to proactive monitoring and early intervention. Instead of responding to deterioration after it becomes clinically obvious, clinicians can anticipate exacerbations, detect subtle progression, and intervene earlier, often outside traditional care settings.

This chapter explores how AI supports disease monitoring and progression tracking across the healthcare continuum. It examines continuous patient monitoring systems, AI-driven alerts for disease exacerbations, remote biometric and sensor integration, clinician-facing dashboards, and the critical distinction between consumer-grade and clinical-grade monitoring technologies.

Continuous Patient Monitoring Systems

Continuous patient monitoring systems represent a fundamental shift in how health and disease are observed and managed. Traditional healthcare models are built around episodic encounters such as clinic visits, hospital admissions, or scheduled follow-ups, in which clinicians assess patients based on a limited snapshot in time. While effective for acute issues, this approach is poorly suited for conditions that evolve gradually or fluctuate daily.

From Episodic Observation to Continuous Insight

Continuous monitoring replaces snapshots with streams. Instead of asking how a patient is doing at a single moment, these systems observe how health changes over days, weeks, and months. This shift is particularly important in chronic and progressive diseases, where early signs of deterioration often appear long before patients feel unwell enough to seek care.

Historical Roots in Acute Care

Historically, continuous monitoring was confined almost exclusively to high-acuity settings such as intensive care units and operating rooms. Patients were connected to bedside monitors that tracked heart rate, blood pressure, oxygen saturation, respiratory rate, and, sometimes, invasive parameters such as arterial pressure.

These systems were effective but resource-intensive, requiring specialized equipment, constant supervision, and physical tethering to clinical environments.

Advances in sensor miniaturization, wireless connectivity, cloud computing, and artificial intelligence have radically expanded the scope of continuous monitoring.

Today, patients can be monitored remotely using wearable devices, implantable sensors, home-based equipment, and mobile health technologies. Monitoring is no longer limited to the sickest patients in hospitals. It increasingly follows individuals into their daily lives.

Multidimensional Data Streams

Modern continuous patient monitoring systems integrate multiple categories of data, creating a richer and more realistic picture of health:

- Physiological signals, such as heart rate, heart rate variability, oxygen saturation, respiratory rate, blood pressure, and glucose levels.
- Behavioral data, including physical activity, sleep duration and quality, sedentary time, and adherence to treatment plans.
- Environmental context, such as ambient temperature, air quality, altitude, or noise exposure, which may influence symptoms or disease control.
- Patient-reported outcomes, including pain, fatigue, breathlessness, mood, or functional limitations, captured through brief digital questionnaires.

Artificial intelligence plays a central role in synthesizing these heterogeneous data streams. Raw sensor outputs are noisy, high-volume, and difficult to interpret in isolation. AI models transform them into meaningful indicators that reflect disease status, trends, and trajectory, distinguishing clinically relevant change from normal day-to-day variation.

Early Detection in Chronic Disease Management

One of the most valuable applications of continuous monitoring is in chronic disease care, where delayed recognition of deterioration is a persistent problem. Many exacerbations are preceded by subtle physiological and behavioral changes that unfold gradually and may not be noticed by patients or clinicians.

In heart failure, for example, early warning signs often include a gradual increase in resting heart rate, reduced daily activity, poorer sleep, and small but consistent weight gain due to fluid retention. Individually, these changes may appear insignificant. AI models trained on longitudinal data can recognize their combined pattern and flag increased risk of decompensation days before hospitalization would otherwise occur.

In diabetes, continuous glucose monitoring data allows AI systems to identify increasing glucose variability, frequent nocturnal hyperglycemia, or delayed recovery after meals - signals of declining metabolic control that may not be captured by periodic HbA1c testing.

In asthma and chronic obstructive pulmonary disease, changes in respiratory rate, reduced activity tolerance, increased rescue inhaler use, or sleep disruption may indicate rising airway inflammation. AI systems can detect these trends early and prompt medication adjustments or clinical review, preventing severe exacerbations.

By enabling earlier intervention, through medication changes, behavioral guidance, or outpatient follow-up, continuous monitoring reduces emergency visits, hospitalizations, and overall disease burden.

Extending Monitoring Beyond Physiology

Importantly, AI-driven monitoring extends beyond traditional vital signs to include functional and behavioral indicators that reflect real-world health impact. These signals often provide earlier and more sensitive markers of decline than physiological measures alone.

For older adults, changes in gait speed, balance, activity patterns, or time spent sedentary may signal declining mobility, increased fall risk, or early frailty. AI systems can detect gradual declines that might otherwise be dismissed as "normal aging."

In neurological conditions, subtle alterations in speech cadence, typing rhythm, facial expression, or movement symmetry may precede clinically obvious progression in disorders such as Parkinson's disease or multiple sclerosis. While these applications are still emerging, they illustrate how AI can detect disease impact on daily function long before traditional clinical assessments.

Toward a Holistic View of Health

By broadening the definition of monitoring, AI enables a more holistic and patient-centered understanding of disease. Health is no longer defined solely by laboratory values or clinic measurements, but by how individuals function, move, sleep, and feel in their everyday environments.

Continuous patient monitoring systems do not replace clinical evaluation; rather, they provide context between visits, supporting earlier recognition of change and more personalized care. When implemented thoughtfully, they transform monitoring from passive observation into an active partnership - one that aligns healthcare delivery with the lived experience of patients over time.

AI Alerts for Disease Exacerbations

Continuous patient monitoring generates a vast amount of data, but data alone does not improve health outcomes. The clinical value of monitoring lies in its ability to trigger timely and appropriate intervention. AI-driven alert systems serve as the critical link between ongoing data collection and meaningful clinical action by identifying patterns associated with disease exacerbation and notifying the right stakeholders at the right time.

From Passive Data Collection to Timely Action

Traditional monitoring systems rely heavily on threshold-based alerts, which activate when a single parameter exceeds a predefined limit, such as heart rate above a certain value or oxygen saturation below a fixed cutoff. While simple to implement, these systems often lack nuance. They do not account for individual baselines, normal daily variability, or interactions between multiple signals. As a result, they may trigger alerts that are either too late or clinically irrelevant.

AI-driven alert systems move beyond this limitation by using context-aware, pattern-based reasoning. Rather than reacting to isolated measurements, AI models analyze trends over time, relationships between variables, and deviations from an individual's usual patterns.

This shift enables earlier and more precise identification of deterioration.

Pattern Recognition and Individualized Risk Signals

One of the defining features of AI alerts is their ability to integrate multiple data streams into a single risk assessment.

For example, in heart failure monitoring, a meaningful alert may be generated not by a single weight change but by a constellation of changes occurring together over several days, such as:

- Gradual weight gain, suggesting fluid retention
- Reduced daily step count, indicating declining functional capacity
- Elevated resting heart rate reflecting increased cardiac stress
- Increased nocturnal awakenings, pointing to worsening symptoms

Individually, each signal may fall within acceptable limits. Together, they form a pattern that AI models recognize as predictive of impending decompensation. Importantly, these models are trained on longitudinal data, allowing them to learn what constitutes meaningful change for each individual rather than relying on population-level averages.

Similar approaches are used in other chronic conditions. In diabetes, AI alerts may combine rising glucose variability, delayed post-meal recovery, and reduced physical activity to identify declining metabolic control. In asthma, increased nighttime symptoms, changes in respiratory rate, and rising rescue inhaler use may collectively signal an exacerbation before severe symptoms develop.

By learning which combinations of signals matter for each patient, AI improves both sensitivity (early detection of true exacerbations) and specificity (avoiding unnecessary alerts).

Reducing False Alarms and Alert Fatigue

Alert fatigue is one of the most significant barriers to effective monitoring. When clinicians or patients are exposed to frequent, low-value alerts, they may become desensitized and ignore warnings, including those that signal genuine risk. This phenomenon undermines trust and can negate the benefits of monitoring systems.

AI addresses alert fatigue through several mechanisms:

- Personalized thresholds, where alert criteria are tailored to an individual's baseline physiology and behavior rather than fixed cutoffs.
- Urgency stratification, which ranks alerts based on clinical significance, allowing users to focus attention where it is most needed.
- Noise suppression, where transient or low-risk deviations, such as brief heart rate elevations during exercise, are filtered out.
- Convergent escalation, where alerts are triggered only when multiple independent indicators point to rising risk.

For example, a temporary increase in heart rate during physical activity would not generate an alert. However, a sustained elevation during rest combined with declining activity and worsening sleep would prompt attention. This layered approach reduces unnecessary interruptions while preserving early warning capability.

Patient-Facing Alerts and Self-Management

Not all alerts require clinician involvement. Many AI systems are designed to support patient-facing alerts that encourage timely self-management. These alerts are typically phrased in supportive, actionable language and aligned with established care plans.

For instance, a patient with asthma may receive a prompt to increase preventive inhaler use, review trigger avoidance strategies, or monitor symptoms more closely. A patient with diabetes may be reminded to adjust their diet, increase physical activity, or check their blood glucose more frequently. These interventions empower patients to take corrective action early, often preventing escalation.

Effective patient-facing alerts are designed to be clear, non-alarmist, and customizable, allowing individuals to control frequency and preferred communication channels.

Clinician and Care Team Alerts

When risk exceeds predefined thresholds or persists despite self-management, alerts are escalated to clinicians or care teams. Clinician-facing alerts may trigger outreach, medication review, diagnostic testing, or scheduling of follow-up visits. Care coordination alerts may notify nurses, case managers, or community health workers to intervene.

Clear escalation pathways are essential. AI systems must define who is notified, how quickly, and what actions are expected. Without such a structure, alerts risk creating ambiguity rather than facilitating care.

From Alerts to Actionable Care

The ultimate goal of AI-driven alert systems is not to generate notifications, but to enable timely, appropriate intervention. When designed thoughtfully, these systems transform continuous monitoring into proactive care by anticipating disease exacerbations, reducing emergency visits, and improving quality of life.

By aligning alerts with individual risk patterns, clinical workflows, and patient capabilities, AI helps ensure that warnings are meaningful, trusted, and acted upon, thus turning data into decisions that make a tangible difference in disease management.

Remote Biometrics and Sensor Integration

Remote disease monitoring is built upon a rapidly expanding ecosystem of biometric sensors embedded in wearable devices, implantable technologies, home-based medical equipment, and mobile platforms. These sensors enable continuous or near-continuous measurement of physiological and behavioral parameters without requiring frequent in-person clinical encounters. As healthcare shifts toward outpatient, home-based, and hybrid care models, remote biometrics have become a foundational data source for AI-driven monitoring and decision support.

The Expanding Sensor Ecosystem

Common remote biometric inputs include continuous glucose monitoring for diabetes management, home blood pressure monitoring for hypertension, pulse oximetry for respiratory and cardiac conditions, cardiac rhythm monitoring through wearable or implantable devices, respiratory rate tracking, and activity and sleep measurement.

Each of these signals provides valuable information, but their true clinical utility emerges when they are observed longitudinally and interpreted in context.

Artificial intelligence plays a critical role in making this sensor ecosystem clinically usable. Remote sensors differ widely in sampling frequency, data format, accuracy, and noise characteristics. Some generate data every few seconds, while others record intermittent readings.

AI systems align these heterogeneous inputs, normalize differences in resolution and timing, and filter noise to produce coherent representations of health status. Without this computational integration, the sheer volume and inconsistency of remote biometric data would overwhelm both patients and clinicians.

From Isolated Metrics to Integrated Health Signals

Historically, biometric measurements were interpreted in isolation: a blood pressure reading, a glucose value, or a heart rate snapshot. Remote monitoring challenges this paradigm by producing continuous streams rather than isolated points.

AI enables a shift from isolated metrics to integrated health signals that reflect trends, variability, and interactions across systems.

For example, a single elevated blood pressure reading at home may be influenced by stress, posture, or measurement technique. AI models can contextualize that reading by comparing it to an individual's baseline, examining recent activity levels, sleep quality, and medication adherence, and determining whether the change is transient or part of a concerning trend. This contextual interpretation reduces false alarms and improves clinical relevance.

Multimodal Data Fusion

One of AI's most powerful contributions to remote monitoring is multimodal data fusion - the ability to combine diverse data types into unified, interpretable insights. Many diseases are influenced by multiple physiological systems and external factors, making single-sensor monitoring insufficient.

In respiratory disease monitoring, for instance, AI systems may integrate oxygen saturation trends, respiratory rate, physical activity tolerance, environmental air quality data, and patient-reported symptoms such as breathlessness or cough. Each signal, individually, provides limited insight. Together, they allow AI models to detect subtle deterioration in disease control, differentiate between exertional and inflammatory causes of symptoms, and anticipate exacerbations before they become clinically severe.

Similarly, in autoimmune diseases, flare-ups are often triggered by complex interactions between immune activity, stress, sleep disruption, and environmental exposures. Multimodal integration allows AI systems to identify patterns that precede symptom worsening, supporting earlier intervention and more personalized management.

In migraine disorders, combining sleep patterns, activity levels, weather data, and self-reported triggers enables AI to recognize individualized risk profiles and provide anticipatory guidance.

Supporting Precision and Personalization

Multimodal sensor integration also supports personalized medicine. Rather than applying generic thresholds, AI systems learn what constitutes "normal" for each individual across multiple dimensions. A resting heart rate that is concerning for one patient may be entirely normal for another. By learning individual baselines and variability, AI improves both sensitivity and specificity in detecting meaningful change.

This personalization is especially important in chronic disease management, where long-term trends matter more than isolated events. AI-driven integration allows clinicians to understand not only whether a value is abnormal, but whether it represents a meaningful departure from a patient's usual pattern.

Challenges in Sensor Reliability and Data Quality

Despite their promise, remote sensors pose significant challenges for data reliability.

Consumer and even clinical-grade devices are subject to movement artifacts, improper placement, inconsistent use, battery limitations, and connectivity disruptions. Patients may forget to wear devices, remove them during certain activities, or use them incorrectly, resulting in incomplete or misleading data.

AI systems mitigate these challenges through several strategies. Signal validation and anomaly detection algorithms identify readings that are physiologically implausible or inconsistent with surrounding data. Redundancy across multiple data streams allows systems to cross-check signals, for example, correlating heart rate with activity level to assess plausibility. Learning individual usage patterns helps distinguish between true physiological change and changes caused by device nonadherence. Intelligent imputation techniques estimate missing data based on historical patterns, reducing gaps without overstating certainty.

However, AI cannot fully eliminate uncertainty. Poor data quality may still obscure clinically relevant signals or generate misleading insights. For this reason, human oversight remains essential.

Clinicians must understand the limitations of sensor-derived data and interpret AI outputs within the broader clinical context.

Toward Reliable, Scalable Remote Monitoring

Remote biometrics and sensor integration represent a cornerstone of AI-enabled disease monitoring. When thoughtfully designed, these systems transform fragmented sensor readings into actionable insights that support early intervention, personalization, and continuity of care. Their success depends on robust integration, transparent handling of uncertainty, and close alignment with clinical workflows. As sensor technology continues to evolve, AI will remain essential in ensuring that more data leads not to more confusion, but to better understanding and better care.

Chronic Disease Dashboards for Clinicians

One of the greatest risks introduced by continuous patient monitoring is not a lack of information, but an excess of it. Wearables, remote sensors, patient-reported outcomes, and automated alerts can generate thousands of data points per patient each week. While this richness holds enormous potential, it is neither feasible nor desirable for clinicians to review raw data streams or daily summaries for large patient populations.

Transforming Continuous Data into Clinical Insight

AI-powered chronic disease dashboards are designed to solve this problem by transforming high-volume, heterogeneous data into clinically meaningful insight. Rather than functioning as data repositories, these dashboards act as interpretive layers that distill complex information into concise, prioritized views aligned with clinical workflows.

Effective dashboards typically present a structured overview that includes:

- Disease trajectories over time, highlighting trends rather than isolated measurements
- Risk scores or stratification levels indicating the likelihood of deterioration or exacerbation
- Alert history and clinician response, providing continuity and accountability
- Adherence and engagement metrics, such as device usage, medication compliance, or symptom reporting
- Comparative benchmarks, allowing clinicians to contextualize an individual's status against similar patients

Crucially, dashboards do not aim to show everything. They emphasize what has changed, why it matters, and what action may be appropriate. For example, instead of displaying daily glucose values for a patient with diabetes, a dashboard may highlight increasing variability over the past two weeks, declining adherence to monitoring, and a rising risk score for poor glycemic control.

Visualizing Disease Progression Over Time

Visualization plays a central role in the effectiveness of dashboards. AI-driven dashboards often use trend lines, color coding, and summaries that allow clinicians to quickly grasp disease progression. Subtle yet persistent changes, such as gradual functional decline or increasing symptom burden, become visible over time.

In heart failure management, for example, a dashboard may display trends in activity levels, resting heart rate, weight, and sleep quality alongside a composite risk indicator. A clinician can immediately see whether the patient is stable, improving, or drifting toward decompensation without reviewing raw data.

Similarly, in chronic kidney disease, dashboards may visualize trends in estimated glomerular filtration rate, blood pressure control, and medication adherence, helping clinicians anticipate progression and plan timely interventions.

Supporting Population Health Management

Beyond individual patient care, chronic disease dashboards are powerful tools for population health management. Care teams responsible for hundreds or thousands of patients cannot rely on manual review to identify those who need attention most urgently. AI-enabled dashboards allow patients to be stratified by risk, enabling proactive and efficient care delivery.

At the population level, dashboards may categorize patients into tiers, such as high risk, moderate risk, and stable. High-risk patients may be flagged for immediate outreach, medication review, or care coordination. Stable patients may continue with routine monitoring and automated support. This risk-based prioritization ensures that limited clinical resources are directed where they can have the greatest impact.

Dashboards also reveal patterns across populations. For example, a care team may observe that patients with a certain comorbidity or social risk factor experience more frequent exacerbations, prompting the redesign of care pathways or targeted interventions. In resource-constrained settings, such insights are critical for scaling chronic disease management without compromising quality.

Integrating Dashboards into Clinical Workflows

For dashboards to be effective, they must integrate seamlessly into existing clinical workflows.

Systems that require clinicians to log into separate platforms or navigate complex interfaces are unlikely to be adopted consistently. Successful dashboards are embedded within electronic health records or care management tools, presenting insights at the point of decision-making.

AI-driven prioritization further reduces cognitive burden by drawing attention to patients or trends that require action, rather than requiring clinicians to search for problems. This "management by exception" approach aligns with the realities of clinical practice.

Decision Support, Not Clinical Automation

It is essential to emphasize that chronic disease dashboards are designed to support - not replace - clinical judgment. AI may suggest that a patient is at increased risk or recommend potential actions, but the clinician remains responsible for interpretation, confirmation, and decision-making.

Transparency is a key design principle. Effective dashboards clearly explain why alerts or risk scores were generated, which variables contributed to them, and how confident the system is in its assessment. Clinicians must be able to drill down into underlying data when needed, especially in complex or ambiguous cases.

This transparency fosters trust and allows clinicians to apply contextual knowledge that AI systems lack, such as patient preferences, recent life events, or nuances not captured in data streams.

Enhancing Care Team Collaboration

Dashboards also support collaboration across multidisciplinary care teams. Nurses, case managers, pharmacists, and physicians can share a common view of patient status, thus improving coordination and reducing duplication of effort. Clear documentation of alerts and responses enhances continuity and accountability across transitions of care.

From Data to Decisions

Chronic disease dashboards represent a critical interface between AI-driven monitoring and human decision-making. By synthesizing continuous data into actionable insight, they help clinicians manage complexity, prioritize care, and intervene earlier.

When thoughtfully designed and transparently implemented, dashboards transform data overload into informed, efficient, and patient-centered care, without displacing the central role of clinical expertise.

Consumer-Grade vs. Clinical-Grade Monitoring

Not all monitoring technologies are created equal. A critical distinction exists between consumer-grade and clinical-grade monitoring systems, particularly when AI-driven insights influence medical decisions.

- Consumer-grade devices prioritize accessibility, engagement, and wellness insights.
- Clinical-grade systems prioritize accuracy, reliability, validation, and regulatory compliance.

While consumer devices play an important role in health engagement and early signal detection, they are not always suitable for diagnostic or treatment decisions.

Accuracy, Validation, and Regulation

Clinical-grade monitoring systems undergo rigorous validation to ensure measurement accuracy across populations and conditions. They are subject to regulatory oversight and quality standards.

Consumer-grade devices may vary widely in performance depending on user characteristics, device placement, and environmental factors. AI can improve signal interpretation, but it cannot fully compensate for hardware limitations.

Bridging the Gap

Increasingly, hybrid models are emerging in which consumer-grade data is used for screening, engagement, and trend detection, while clinical-grade systems confirm findings and guide treatment.

Clear communication about limitations is essential to prevent misuse and misinterpretation.

Conclusion

AI-enabled disease monitoring and progression tracking represent a fundamental shift in healthcare delivery. By extending insight beyond clinic walls, AI supports earlier detection of deterioration, personalized intervention, and more efficient use of resources.

However, technology alone is insufficient. Successful monitoring requires thoughtful integration into workflows, clear escalation pathways, ethical governance, and sustained patient engagement.

When implemented responsibly, AI-driven monitoring transforms disease management from episodic observation to continuous partnership - one that aligns clinical care with the realities of how disease unfolds in daily life.

Chapter 8: Virtual Health Assistance and Chatbots: The Rise of Conversational Care

Healthcare has long struggled with a paradox: while patient needs are continuous, access to clinicians is episodic, constrained by time, staffing, and cost. Patients experience symptoms at night, need reassurance between visits, forget instructions, and navigate complex systems with limited guidance.

Traditional care models were never designed to support this level of ongoing interaction.

Virtual health assistants and AI-powered chatbots have emerged as a response to this gap. Enabled by advances in artificial intelligence, particularly natural language processing (NLP), machine learning, and conversational interfaces, these systems provide scalable, always-available support across the healthcare continuum. They engage patients outside clinical settings, answer questions, guide navigation, reinforce care plans, and escalate concerns when human intervention is needed.

Importantly, virtual health assistants are not intended to replace clinicians. Their value lies in augmenting healthcare delivery by handling routine interactions, improving access to information, and supporting continuity of care. When designed responsibly, they reduce friction, enhance patient experience, and free clinicians to focus on complex, high-value tasks.

This chapter explores how AI-driven virtual assistants function, where they are most effective, and what safeguards are necessary to ensure safety, trust, and ethical use.

Patient Engagement Platforms

Patient engagement has traditionally been mediated through relatively passive tools such as patient portals, appointment reminders, and static educational materials. While these systems improved access to health information and facilitated basic communication, they often failed to sustain meaningful engagement over time.

Patients were expected to log in, search for information, and initiate contact, placing the burden of engagement largely on the individual. As a result, many patients interacted with these tools only intermittently, limiting their impact on outcomes.

From Portals to Proactive Engagement

AI-powered virtual assistants represent a significant evolution from this model. Rather than serving as passive repositories, these systems enable proactive engagement by initiating interactions, monitoring patient status, and responding dynamically to user input. Embedded within mobile applications, patient portals, messaging platforms, or voice-based interfaces, virtual assistants create ongoing conversational relationships that extend care beyond traditional clinical encounters.

For example, after hospital discharge, a virtual assistant may check in daily to assess symptoms, pain levels, or medication tolerance. If a patient reports worsening shortness of breath or increasing pain, the system can prompt further questions, provide guidance, or escalate concerns to a care team.

This approach helps identify complications early, reducing readmissions and improving patient confidence during vulnerable transitions of care.

Similarly, virtual assistants routinely support medication adherence by delivering reminders, answering dosing questions, and identifying barriers such as side effects or confusion. For chronic disease management, assistants may ask structured questions to monitor control, such as tracking blood pressure trends in hypertension or symptom frequency in asthma, and provide real-time guidance when patients report concerns.

Importantly, these interactions occur asynchronously, allowing patients to engage at their convenience rather than within limited clinic hours. This flexibility aligns more closely with real-world patient needs and improves accessibility for individuals managing work, caregiving, or mobility challenges.

Personalization at Scale

One of the defining advantages of AI-driven engagement platforms is their ability to deliver personalization at scale.

Traditional engagement strategies often rely on generic messaging, which may feel irrelevant or overwhelming to patients. AI systems, by contrast, adapt tone, frequency, and content based on individual behavior, preferences, and health status.

For a patient managing hypertension, a virtual assistant may focus on blood pressure trends, reinforce medication adherence, and offer lifestyle guidance related to diet, exercise, and stress management. If the patient consistently engages with dietary tips but ignores exercise prompts, the system may adjust its emphasis accordingly. For a patient undergoing cancer treatment, interactions may center on symptom monitoring, side-effect management, appointment coordination, and emotional support, reflecting the patient's evolving needs.

Machine learning models refine engagement strategies over time by learning which messages prompt responses, which interventions improve adherence, and when escalation is necessary. This adaptive approach prevents message fatigue and ensures that engagement remains relevant rather than repetitive.

Reducing Care Gaps and Missed Opportunities

AI-powered patient engagement platforms are particularly effective in reducing care gaps, especially missed appointments, incomplete follow-ups, delayed testing, and unreported symptoms that compromise outcomes. By maintaining continuous, low-friction contact, these systems act as a safety net between visits.

For example, if a patient misses a follow-up appointment, the virtual assistant can proactively reach out to reschedule, clarify barriers, or provide interim guidance. If laboratory tests are overdue, reminders can be delivered in a timely and supportive manner. When patients report symptoms that would otherwise go unaddressed until the next visit, early intervention becomes possible.

In population health programs, these platforms help ensure that preventive care measures, such as vaccinations, screenings, or chronic disease check-ins, are completed. By systematically identifying and addressing gaps, AI-driven engagement improves continuity and equity of care.

Enhancing Patient Confidence and Self-Efficacy

Beyond logistics, patient engagement platforms support self-efficacy by reinforcing understanding and confidence. Patients who feel supported between visits are more likely to adhere to care plans and seek help when needed. Virtual assistants provide reassurance, clarify instructions, and normalize common experiences, reducing anxiety and uncertainty.

By offering consistent, personalized support, AI-powered engagement platforms transform patient interaction from sporadic contact to an ongoing relationship. When designed thoughtfully, they strengthen continuity of care, reduce preventable complications, and create a more responsive, patient-centered healthcare experience that meets individuals where they are, both clinically and in daily life.

Natural Language Interfaces for Health Queries

One of the most transformative advances in virtual health assistance is the use of natural language interfaces. Traditionally, digital health tools required patients to navigate rigid menus, select from predefined symptom lists, or complete structured forms. While these approaches ensured data consistency, they often felt cumbersome and failed to reflect how people naturally describe their health concerns.

From Forms to Conversations

Natural language interfaces shift this interaction from form-filling to conversation. Patients can type or speak in their own words, expressing symptoms, concerns, or questions as they would to a clinician. This conversational approach lowers barriers to engagement, reduces frustration, and captures richer clinical information.

Natural language processing (NLP) enables virtual assistants to interpret free-text input and spoken language by:

- Extracting clinically relevant symptom descriptions
- Recognizing user intent, such as seeking general information versus reporting a concerning symptom
- Handling variations in phrasing, slang, abbreviations, or misspellings
- Maintaining conversational context across multiple turns

For example, a patient might say, “I’ve been feeling dizzy since yesterday, and my heart feels fast,” rather than selecting checkboxes for dizziness and palpitations. An NLP system identifies key clinical concepts, recognizes temporal information, and prompts appropriate follow-up questions.

This mirrors the early stages of a clinical interview while remaining accessible and user-friendly.

Understanding Intent and Context

Effective natural language interfaces go beyond keyword recognition. They are designed to understand intent - what the user is trying to accomplish - and context - how current input relates to previous exchanges.

A user asking, “Is it normal to feel tired after starting this medication?” requires a different response than someone saying, “I feel extremely weak and can’t get out of bed.” Both mention fatigue, but the intent and urgency differ. NLP systems analyze language cues, sentence structure, and prior conversation history to distinguish between routine information-seeking and potential clinical concern.

Maintaining context across multiple interactions is equally important. If a patient has already reported a diagnosis or medication earlier in the conversation, the system should incorporate that information into subsequent responses. This continuity creates a more natural and efficient interaction and avoids repetitive questioning.

Handling Complexity and Ambiguity in Health Queries

Health-related queries are often vague, emotionally charged, or incomplete. Patients may struggle to articulate symptoms, use non-medical language, or focus on sensations rather than clinically precise descriptions. AI systems must navigate this ambiguity carefully to avoid misinterpretation or inappropriate reassurance.

Effective virtual assistants use adaptive questioning to clarify meaning step by step. Rather than presenting long, overwhelming questionnaires, they ask targeted follow-up questions based on initial input. These may explore duration, severity, associated symptoms, triggers, or relevant medical history.

For example, if a patient reports chest discomfort, the system may ask whether the sensation is sharp or pressure-like, whether it occurs at rest or with activity, and whether it is associated with shortness of breath or nausea.

This approach mirrors aspects of clinical reasoning while remaining concise and respectful of user time.

Importantly, adaptive questioning is designed to balance thoroughness with user experience. Overly aggressive probing can feel intrusive or alarming, while insufficient clarification can lead to unsafe recommendations. Well-designed systems adjust their depth based on perceived risk and user responses.

Emotional Sensitivity and Language Tone

Natural language interfaces also play a role in recognizing emotional cues. Words expressing fear, frustration, or distress may signal heightened anxiety or unmet needs. While AI cannot replicate human empathy, it can acknowledge emotions and respond in a supportive, non-dismissive manner.

For example, a response that begins with "I'm sorry you're feeling this way" or "That sounds uncomfortable" helps validate the user's experience and builds trust. Such language choices are essential in maintaining engagement and encouraging honest communication.

Multilingual and Accessibility Benefits

Natural language interfaces significantly improve accessibility across diverse populations. Multilingual support allows patients to interact in their preferred language, reducing miscommunication and enhancing inclusivity. This is particularly important in regions with linguistic diversity or among migrant populations.

Voice-based interfaces further expand accessibility for individuals with limited literacy, visual impairment, or motor challenges that make typing difficult. By enabling spoken interaction, AI-powered assistants reach users who may otherwise be excluded from digital health tools.

These capabilities are especially valuable in underserved populations, where traditional digital platforms may be less effective due to literacy barriers, limited health education, or lack of familiarity with complex interfaces.

Expanding Reach Without Sacrificing Safety

By allowing patients to communicate naturally, natural language interfaces make virtual health assistance more intuitive, inclusive, and scalable. However, these systems must be carefully designed with safety in mind. Clear boundaries, escalation protocols, and transparency about limitations are essential to ensure that conversational ease does not lead to false reassurance.

When implemented responsibly, natural language interfaces transform health queries from rigid transactions into meaningful conversations, making healthcare support more accessible, responsive, and aligned with how people actually communicate about their health.

AI Agents in Scheduling, Refills, and Education

A substantial proportion of healthcare interactions involve administrative and logistical tasks rather than direct clinical decision-making.

Activities such as scheduling appointments, requesting prescription refills, confirming instructions, and checking the status of tests or referrals are essential to care continuity, yet they consume significant staff time and often create friction for patients. Delays, unanswered calls, and fragmented communication can lead to missed care, frustration, and avoidable clinical risk.

AI-powered agents are particularly well-suited to these domains.

Automating Administrative Tasks to Reduce Friction

Virtual assistants can handle routine administrative workflows efficiently and consistently, operating around the clock and reducing dependency on call centers or manual processing. Common functions include scheduling, rescheduling, or canceling appointments; sending reminders and confirmations; processing prescription refill requests; and providing updates on laboratory results or referral status.

In integrated healthcare systems, these agents connect directly to electronic health records, scheduling platforms, and pharmacy systems. This integration enables seamless execution rather than manual handoffs.

For example, a patient requesting a refill through a virtual assistant can have the request automatically verified against medication history, refill eligibility, and recent clinical notes before being routed appropriately, either approved automatically or escalated to a clinician or pharmacist when review is required.

Improving Access and Efficiency

Automating administrative tasks improves both patient access and operational efficiency. Patients can schedule appointments or request refills at their convenience, without navigating phone trees or waiting for office hours. Clinicians and staff, in turn, are freed from repetitive tasks and can focus on complex care needs that require human judgment.

For example, a virtual assistant may identify appointment availability based on patient preferences, insurance constraints, and clinical urgency, offering suitable options in real time. In high-volume practices, this reduces no-show rates and improves utilization of clinical resources.

Medication Management and Adherence Support

Medication adherence remains one of the most persistent challenges in healthcare, particularly for chronic conditions requiring long-term therapy. Nonadherence can result from forgetfulness, side effects, cost barriers, misunderstanding of instructions, or lack of perceived benefit. AI-driven virtual assistants support adherence by combining reminders with contextual understanding.

Rather than issuing generic alerts, AI agents adapt reminders based on patient behavior and response patterns. If a patient consistently takes medication late, the system may adjust reminder timing or ask whether schedule changes are needed. If refills are repeatedly delayed, the assistant may inquire about side effects, affordability, or confusion regarding dosing.

For example, a patient managing hypertension who frequently postpones refills may be prompted with a brief check-in: "I noticed your refill is overdue. Are you experiencing side effects, or would you like help with a refill?" Depending on the response, the system can escalate to a pharmacist or clinician to address underlying barriers.

This approach transforms adherence support from passive reminders into an interactive problem-solving approach.

Safe Escalation and Oversight

Importantly, AI agents are designed with clear escalation rules. Requests that fall outside predefined safety parameters, such as early refills of controlled substances or medication changes, are routed to human review. This ensures that automation enhances efficiency without compromising safety or regulatory compliance.

Health Education and Self-Management Support

Education is another core function of AI-driven virtual assistants. Patients often receive large volumes of information during clinical encounters, much of which is difficult to retain or apply. Virtual assistants reinforce learning by delivering personalized, timely educational content aligned with diagnosis, treatment stage, and individual learning preferences.

Rather than providing lengthy documents or static links, AI systems deliver information in digestible segments over time. For example, a patient newly diagnosed with diabetes may receive step-by-step guidance on glucose monitoring, dietary choices, physical activity, and symptom recognition, with each topic introduced gradually and reinforced through interactive questions.

Education becomes a dialogue rather than a one-time event. Patients can ask follow-up questions, clarify instructions, and receive feedback tailored to their responses. This interactive approach improves comprehension, retention, and self-efficacy.

Supporting Long-Term Engagement

By integrating scheduling, medication management, and education into a single conversational interface, AI agents reduce fragmentation and support sustained engagement. Patients interact with a consistent system that understands their history, preferences, and needs, creating a sense of continuity.

When implemented thoughtfully, AI agents in scheduling, refills, and education reduce administrative burden, improve adherence, and empower patients to manage their health more effectively. They exemplify how AI can enhance everyday healthcare interactions - not by replacing clinicians, but by removing friction and reinforcing care between visits.

Emotional Intelligence and Patient Support

Healthcare interactions are never purely informational. Patients bring emotions into every encounter - anxiety about symptoms, fear of diagnosis, frustration with treatment complexity, and uncertainty about outcomes. These emotional states influence how individuals interpret information, adhere to recommendations, and engage with care.

As virtual health assistants become more integrated into everyday healthcare, their ability to recognize and respond appropriately to emotional cues becomes increasingly important.

Recognizing the Emotional Dimension of Care

AI systems are now being designed with elements of emotional intelligence, using techniques such as sentiment analysis, language pattern recognition, and behavioral signal detection to infer emotional states. While these systems do not experience emotions themselves, they can identify patterns that suggest distress, confusion, or disengagement.

For example, repeated late-night messages asking similar questions may indicate anxiety or rumination. Language expressing hopelessness or self-blame may signal emotional distress. Sudden disengagement after an intense interaction may suggest frustration or overwhelm. By recognizing these patterns, AI systems can adapt their responses and escalate support when appropriate.

Responding with Empathy and Validation

Once emotional cues are detected, the system's response matters. A purely factual reply to an emotionally charged message can feel dismissive and undermine trust. Effective virtual assistants acknowledge emotions explicitly, using supportive and validating language before offering information or guidance.

For instance, responding with "That sounds worrying, and it's understandable to feel concerned" helps normalize the patient's experience. This validation does not require clinical judgment, but it signals attentiveness and care. Following this, the system can provide relevant information or suggest next steps in a calm, reassuring manner.

Such emotionally aware responses improve user engagement and encourage continued communication, which is especially important for individuals who may hesitate to seek help due to fear or stigma.

Supporting Mental and Emotional Well-Being

Beyond recognition and validation, AI-powered assistants can offer structured support for emotional well-being.

In non-crisis contexts, virtual assistants may guide users through simple stress-reduction techniques, breathing exercises, or grounding strategies. For patients managing chronic illness, reminders to rest, reflect on progress, or acknowledge effort can reinforce resilience and self-efficacy.

In mental health care, AI chatbots are increasingly used to support evidence-based approaches such as cognitive behavioral techniques. These systems may help users track mood, identify thought patterns, and practice coping strategies between therapy sessions. While they are not substitutes for professional care, they can provide accessible, low-intensity support that complements human intervention.

Importantly, emotionally intelligent systems must remain conservative in their scope. They are designed to support, not diagnose or treat mental health conditions independently.

Knowing When to Escalate to Human Support

A critical aspect of emotional intelligence in AI is knowing when to escalate. When signs of significant distress, suicidal ideation, or crisis emerge, the system must shift from supportive messaging to prompt connection with human support.

This may include encouraging contact with a clinician, mental health professional, or crisis line, and providing clear instructions for immediate help when necessary. Escalation protocols must be carefully designed, tested, and transparent to ensure safety and reliability.

For example, if a user expresses feelings of hopelessness combined with statements suggesting self-harm, the system should prioritize safety by acknowledging distress and directing the individual to appropriate human resources without delay.

Building Trust Through Tone and Transparency

Tone is a powerful determinant of trust. Overly clinical language can feel impersonal and alienating, while excessively casual language may undermine credibility. Effective AI systems strike a careful balance between empathy, respect, and clarity, without overstepping professional boundaries.

Transparency further reinforces trust. Acknowledging system limitations, such as stating "I may not have all the information" or "This doesn't replace talking to a healthcare professional", signals humility and encourages users to seek additional help when needed. Rather than eroding confidence, such honesty enhances credibility and supports informed decision-making.

Ethical Considerations and Responsible Design

Emotionally responsive AI must be designed ethically. Systems should avoid manipulating emotions, fostering dependency, or presenting themselves as substitutes for human relationships. Users should always be aware that they are interacting with an AI system, and consent to the processing of emotional data must be explicit.

When implemented responsibly, emotional intelligence in virtual health assistants enhances patient support without overreaching. By recognizing emotional context, responding with empathy, and escalating appropriately, AI systems can strengthen patient engagement, reduce isolation, and support emotional well-being, while preserving the essential role of human care.

Reliability, Liability, and Escalation Protocols

As virtual health assistants become more deeply embedded in clinical workflows and patient-facing care pathways, reliability and safety become non-negotiable requirements. Unlike general consumer chatbots, healthcare-focused AI systems operate in environments where incorrect guidance, delayed escalation, or misunderstood recommendations can lead to real harm.

Ensuring Safe and Appropriate Use

Safe design begins with clearly defining the scope of use. Well-designed systems explicitly distinguish between informational support (such as general education), decision guidance (such as triage recommendations), and situations that require immediate human intervention. For example, a virtual assistant may provide lifestyle advice for mild symptoms but must defer to clinicians when symptoms suggest serious or rapidly evolving conditions.

Clear boundaries help manage user expectations and reduce the risk of over-reliance on automated guidance.

Escalation as a Core Design Principle

Escalation protocols are central to the safe operation of virtual health assistants. These protocols define when, how, and to whom concerns are transferred from the AI system to human professionals. Escalation should not be an afterthought but a foundational design feature.

Common triggers for escalation include:

- Red-flag symptoms, such as chest pain, severe shortness of breath, or neurological deficits
- Worsening trends identified through symptom reporting or remote monitoring data
- Expressions of severe emotional distress, including suicidal ideation or extreme anxiety
- Repeated unanswered or unresolved questions, suggesting confusion or unmet needs

For example, if a patient reports worsening pain despite following guidance, the system may escalate to a nurse or clinician for direct follow-up. In urgent scenarios, escalation may include directing the patient to emergency services with clear instructions.

Effective escalation pathways are explicit, timely, and auditable, ensuring that responsibility is clearly transferred and that no alerts are lost or ignored.

Liability and Accountability Considerations

Legal responsibility for AI-assisted interactions remains a complex and evolving area. While AI systems may generate guidance or prompts, accountability ultimately rests with healthcare organizations and licensed professionals who deploy and oversee these tools.

To support accountability, systems must maintain comprehensive audit trails. Virtual assistants should log interactions, recommendations, confidence levels, and escalation decisions. Clear disclaimers reinforce that AI tools are supportive rather than diagnostic and do not replace professional judgment.

These records are essential for quality assurance, regulatory compliance, and review in the event of adverse outcomes.

Monitoring, Evaluation, and Continuous Improvement

Reliability is not static. AI systems must be continuously monitored to ensure they remain accurate, relevant, and safe as clinical guidelines evolve and user behavior changes.

Some key performance metrics may include:

- Accuracy and appropriateness of responses
- Timeliness and suitability of escalations
- User satisfaction and engagement
- Rates of adverse events or near misses

Continuous feedback loops allow organizations to refine algorithms, update escalation criteria, and identify unintended consequences early.

When supported by strong governance and oversight, reliable, well-escalated virtual health assistants can safely enhance access, efficiency, and continuity of care while maintaining clear accountability and patient trust.

Conclusion

Virtual health assistants and chatbots represent a foundational shift in how healthcare systems interact with patients. By providing continuous, conversational, and personalized support, they extend care beyond clinical walls and reduce friction in everyday health management.

Their value lies not in replacing clinicians but in amplifying care capacity, improving access, and supporting patients in moments when traditional systems are unavailable.

When designed responsibly, with clear boundaries, ethical safeguards, and human oversight, AI-powered virtual assistants become a trusted layer of care: one that listens, guides, and connects patients to the right support at the right time.

As healthcare continues its transition toward proactive, patient-centered models, virtual health assistance will play an increasingly central role in shaping the experience of treatment and care.

Chapter 9: Emergency Care and Artificial Intelligence

Emergency care represents one of the most demanding environments in healthcare. Emergency departments (EDs) and pre-hospital systems operate under constant time pressure, uncertainty, and resource constraints. Clinicians must make rapid decisions with incomplete information, prioritize patients with varying degrees of urgency, and manage unpredictable surges in demand. Errors or delays can have immediate and severe consequences.

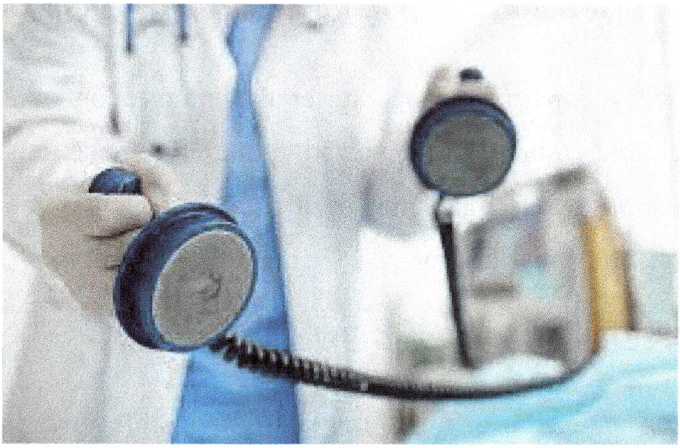

Artificial intelligence is uniquely positioned to support emergency care because it excels at rapid data processing, pattern recognition, and real-time risk assessment.

Unlike many other clinical settings, emergency medicine generates continuous streams of structured and unstructured data, including vital signs, laboratory results, imaging, clinical notes, triage inputs, and monitoring signals, that must be synthesized quickly.

This chapter explores how AI is being applied across the emergency care continuum, from real-time decision support within emergency departments to pre-hospital emergency medical services (EMS), predictive modeling of critical events, and system-level integration to improve time-sensitive outcomes.

Throughout, the emphasis remains on augmentation rather than automation: AI supports clinicians, enhances situational awareness, and improves coordination, while human judgment remains central.

Real-Time Decision Support in Emergency Departments

Emergency departments operate at the intersection of urgency, uncertainty, and volume. Clinicians are required to make rapid, high-stakes decisions while managing frequent interruptions, incomplete information, and simultaneous care for multiple patients.

The Cognitive Burden of Emergency Medicine

A single physician or nurse may be responsible for patients at different stages of evaluation, including triage, diagnosis, treatment, or disposition, each with evolving clinical needs. Under these conditions, cognitive overload is a persistent and well-documented risk.

Artificial intelligence-driven real-time decision support systems are designed to help mitigate this burden.

Rather than attempting to replace clinical judgment, these systems function as an additional layer of vigilance. They continuously analyze incoming data streams in the background, synthesizing information that would otherwise require sustained human attention, and highlight signals that warrant closer review.

In doing so, AI supports situational awareness without demanding constant manual surveillance.

Continuous Data Synthesis in High-Throughput Settings

Modern emergency departments generate vast amounts of real-time data. Vital signs are updated minute by minute, laboratory results arrive asynchronously, imaging studies produce preliminary and final reports, and clinicians document assessments and plans under time pressure.

Monitoring data from telemetry, pulse oximetry, and bedside devices further adds to the information load.

AI systems integrate these heterogeneous inputs dynamically, updating risk assessments as new information becomes available. For example, a patient initially triaged as low acuity may develop subtle but concerning trends, such as increasing heart rate variability, declining blood pressure, or rising lactate levels, that are difficult to detect in isolation. AI algorithms can identify these evolving patterns and surface them to clinicians before overt instability occurs.

This continuous synthesis allows emergency teams to move from reactive recognition of deterioration to more proactive management.

Clinical Use Cases in Emergency Care

One of the most prominent applications of AI-driven decision support in the ED is sepsis detection.

Sepsis often presents with nonspecific symptoms, and early signs may be subtle. AI systems analyze combinations of vital signs, laboratory markers, and clinical documentation to identify patients at risk hours before traditional criteria are met. Early alerts prompt clinicians to initiate diagnostic testing, fluid resuscitation, and antibiotics sooner, which is associated with improved survival.

In trauma care, AI supports rapid interpretation of imaging and physiological data. For example, computer vision algorithms may assist in identifying internal bleeding on CT scans, while predictive models analyze vital sign trends to flag patients at risk of hemorrhagic shock. These tools help teams prioritize interventions in complex, time-sensitive situations.

AI decision support is also used to identify patients at risk of clinical deterioration, such as impending respiratory failure or cardiac events, enabling earlier escalation of care.

Interpretability and Clinical Trust

For real-time decision support to be effective, interpretability is essential. Clinicians must understand why an alert was generated and which data points contributed to the assessment. Black-box alerts without explanation risk being ignored or mistrusted, particularly in high-pressure environments.

Well-designed systems present alerts with context - highlighting relevant trends, recent changes, and contributing factors - allowing clinicians to rapidly assess validity and act appropriately. When AI augments awareness without undermining autonomy, it becomes a valuable partner in emergency care, enhancing safety, efficiency, and clinical decision-making under pressure.

Triage and Resource Allocation

Emergency department triage has long relied on standardized scoring systems combined with clinician judgment to assign acuity levels and prioritize care. These frameworks, such as color-coded or numerical triage scales, provide a necessary structure in high-volume environments. However, they are inherently limited by static criteria and human variability.

Limitations of Traditional Triage Models

Traditional triage often depends on a snapshot assessment taken at arrival, focusing on presenting complaints and initial vital signs.

Under busy conditions, subtle indicators of severity may be overlooked, and patients with similar symptoms may be assigned the same acuity level despite very different underlying risks. Over-triage can strain already limited resources by directing attention to low-risk patients, while under-triage can delay care for those who are critically ill, increasing the risk of adverse outcomes.

These limitations become more pronounced during periods of crowding, staffing shortages, or surges in patient volume, when rapid decisions must be made with incomplete information.

AI-Enhanced Triage Systems

AI-driven triage systems address these challenges by analyzing a broader and more dynamic set of variables than traditional methods.

Rather than relying solely on presenting complaints and single-point measurements, AI models integrate information such as demographics and comorbidities, free-text symptom descriptions, trends in vital signs, historical healthcare utilization, and prior diagnoses or medications.

By synthesizing these factors, AI systems generate more nuanced risk stratification.

This approach prioritizes patients based on their likelihood of deterioration rather than symptom category alone. For example, two patients may present with chest pain and appear similar during initial triage. An AI system may identify one as higher risk due to advanced age, known coronary artery disease, subtle electrocardiogram changes, and rising cardiac biomarkers, prompting faster evaluation and intervention.

AI-enhanced triage does not replace clinician judgment; instead, it provides an additional layer of insight that supports more informed prioritization under pressure.

Dynamic Resource Allocation Across the Emergency Department

Beyond individual triage decisions, AI plays an increasingly important role in system-level resource allocation. Emergency departments operate as complex systems where patient flow, bed availability, staffing levels, and diagnostic capacity must be continuously balanced.

Predictive AI models analyze historical patterns and real-time data to estimate incoming patient volume, acuity distribution, bed demand, and utilization of imaging and laboratory services. These insights allow administrators and charge nurses to anticipate bottlenecks before they become critical.

For example, during peak periods, AI tools may forecast a surge in high-acuity patients, prompting early adjustments such as calling in additional staff, opening surge treatment areas, or expediting discharges for stable patients. In settings prone to overcrowding, these systems support informed decisions about ambulance diversion or prioritization of specific patient pathways.

Improving Throughput and Patient Safety

By aligning triage decisions with real-time resource management, AI supports both patient safety and operational efficiency. More accurate prioritization reduces delays for high-risk patients, while proactive resource allocation improves throughput and reduces clinician stress.

When implemented thoughtfully, AI-enhanced triage and resource allocation tools help emergency departments respond dynamically to fluctuating demand, ensuring that limited resources are deployed where they can have the greatest impact.

AI-Assisted Pre-Hospital Care (EMS)

Pre-hospital care is the earliest and often most decisive phase of the emergency care continuum. Emergency medical services (EMS) clinicians must make rapid, high-stakes decisions in uncontrolled environments, frequently with limited diagnostic tools, incomplete patient histories, and time pressure.

Choices made in the field, such as transport destination, urgency of care, and early treatment initiation, can significantly influence patient outcomes.

The Expanding Role of AI Before Hospital Arrival

AI-assisted pre-hospital systems extend clinical decision support beyond hospital walls into ambulances and field settings. By analyzing data in real time, these systems help EMS teams recognize critical conditions earlier, reduce diagnostic uncertainty, and coordinate more effectively with receiving facilities.

The result is faster, more targeted care from the moment of first contact.

Decision Support for EMS Providers

AI tools support EMS clinicians by synthesizing multiple sources of information collected in the field. These may include vital signs and continuous monitoring data, electrocardiogram (ECG) readings, mechanism of injury, limited patient history when available, scene context, and estimated transport time.

In cardiac care, AI algorithms play a particularly important role. Automated ECG interpretation systems can identify patterns consistent with ST-elevation myocardial infarction (STEMI) in the pre-hospital setting. When STEMI is detected, AI-supported alerts enable EMS teams to bypass non-specialized facilities and transport patients directly to cardiac catheterization centers. Simultaneously, interventional cardiology teams can be activated before arrival, reducing door-to-balloon times and improving survival.

In stroke care, AI-supported assessment tools assist EMS providers in estimating stroke severity using structured clinical inputs and, in some regions, portable imaging or advanced neurological assessments. These tools help determine whether patients should be transported to primary stroke centers or comprehensive stroke centers capable of mechanical thrombectomy. Early and appropriate routing is critical, as delays in advanced intervention can result in irreversible neurological damage.

Trauma care also benefits from AI-assisted decision support. By integrating the mechanism of injury, physiological data, and scene characteristics, AI systems can help identify patients who would benefit from transport to trauma centers rather than local hospitals, improving outcomes in severe injury cases.

Operational Coordination and System Readiness

Beyond individual decision support, AI enhances operational coordination between EMS teams and emergency departments. Real-time data transmission from ambulances allows hospitals to receive vital signs, ECGs, and preliminary assessments before the patient arrives.

This early visibility enables emergency departments to mobilize appropriate teams, prepare equipment, and allocate resources proactively.

Predictive models further support coordination by estimating arrival times, anticipated patient acuity, and likely resource needs. For example, if AI predicts that a patient is at high risk of rapid deterioration, the receiving hospital can prepare intensive care resources or specialty teams in advance. This reduces delays at handoff and improves continuity of care.

Improving Outcomes Through Early Intelligence

AI-assisted pre-hospital care strengthens the entire emergency response chain by shifting critical decision-making earlier in the care pathway. When EMS teams are supported by intelligent tools that enhance recognition, routing, and communication, patients receive the right care at the right place sooner.

Importantly, these systems are designed to support EMS clinical judgment. By augmenting situational awareness and reducing uncertainty, AI empowers pre-hospital clinicians to make more informed decisions under pressure, ultimately improving outcomes in time-sensitive emergencies.

Predictive Models for Critical Events

One of the most powerful contributions of artificial intelligence to emergency care is its ability to anticipate critical events *before* they become clinically obvious.

These events, such as cardiac arrest, respiratory failure, septic shock, or sudden hemodynamic collapse, often evolve over time through subtle physiological changes that are difficult for humans to track continuously in high-pressure environments.

Anticipating Deterioration Before It Occurs

Traditional monitoring systems rely heavily on threshold-based alarms. While necessary, these alarms tend to trigger late in the course of deterioration and generate frequent false positives.

Alarm fatigue is a well-recognized consequence, leading clinicians to silence alerts or respond more slowly. AI-driven predictive models address these limitations by analyzing trends, interactions, and deviations from individual baselines rather than reacting to single abnormal values.

By continuously processing multivariate data streams, AI systems can identify early warning signatures that precede overt instability, enabling earlier and more targeted intervention.

Examples of Predictive Applications in Emergency Care

In cardiac monitoring, AI models analyze high-resolution electrocardiogram waveforms, heart rate variability, and rhythm dynamics to predict life-threatening arrhythmias or cardiac arrest minutes to hours in advance. Subtle changes in waveform morphology or variability that are imperceptible to the human eye may signal rising risk. Early alerts allow clinicians to adjust monitoring intensity, prepare medications, or initiate preventive interventions.

In respiratory care, predictive models assess breathing patterns, trends in oxygen saturation, respiratory rate variability, and patient movement. AI systems may detect an increase in breathing rate or a decline in respiratory reserve before oxygen levels fall dramatically.

These early warnings support timely escalation to noninvasive ventilation, respiratory therapy, or transfer to the intensive care unit, potentially preventing respiratory failure.

In trauma and critical illness, AI models integrate vital signs, laboratory values, and injury characteristics to estimate bleeding risk, coagulopathy, or progression toward shock. For example, subtle trends in heart rate, blood pressure, and lactate levels may indicate occult hemorrhage even when initial assessments appear reassuring. Predictive insights support faster decision-making under uncertainty, such as prioritizing imaging, transfusion, or surgical consultation.

Balancing Sensitivity and Specificity

Predictive accuracy in emergency settings must be carefully balanced. Overly sensitive models may generate excessive alerts, overwhelming clinicians and undermining trust. Overly conservative models risk missing early signs of deterioration, negating potential benefits.

Maintaining this balance requires continuous evaluation and recalibration. Models must be tested across diverse patient populations, monitored for performance drift, and refined based on clinician feedback. Importantly, predictive outputs should be presented as risk estimates or trends rather than definitive conclusions, reinforcing their role as decision support rather than directives.

System Integration and Time-Critical Outcomes

In emergency care, time is a decisive factor. Delays of minutes or even seconds can significantly affect survival and long-term outcomes. For AI systems to be effective in this context, they must be deeply integrated into clinical workflows, electronic health records, monitoring platforms, and communication systems.

Standalone tools that require manual data entry or separate logins introduce friction and reduce adoption.

In contrast, successful AI implementations operate largely in the background, continuously analyzing data and surfacing insights directly within systems clinicians already use. Alerts, risk scores, and recommendations must appear at the right moment, in the right place, and in a format that supports rapid interpretation.

Improving Time-to-Treatment Metrics

When seamlessly integrated, AI has demonstrated a measurable impact on critical emergency care metrics. These include reductions in door-to-antibiotic time for sepsis, door-to-balloon time in myocardial infarction, door-to-needle time in stroke, and time to intensive care unit transfer for deteriorating patients.

By accelerating recognition, coordination, and decision-making, AI reduces delays that directly influence morbidity and mortality. Earlier activation of care pathways, faster mobilization of teams, and improved handoffs all contribute to better outcomes.

Governance, Safety, and Accountability

Given the high stakes of emergency care, AI deployment must be supported by robust governance structures. Models should be validated in real-world settings, monitored continuously, and supported by clear escalation and override protocols.

Clinicians must retain ultimate authority, with AI serving as an advisory system rather than an autonomous decision-maker. Transparency, audit trails, and performance monitoring are essential to maintaining trust, accountability, and patient safety in time-critical environments.

Conclusion

Emergency care demands speed, precision, and coordination under uncertainty. Artificial intelligence enhances these capabilities by providing real-time decision support, improving triage accuracy, extending insight into pre-hospital settings, and predicting critical events before they unfold.

When integrated thoughtfully, AI acts as a force multiplier, amplifying human expertise rather than replacing it. Its success depends not only on algorithmic performance but also on workflow integration, clinician trust, ethical governance, and continuous evaluation.

As emergency care systems face increasing demand and complexity, AI will play an increasingly central role in ensuring timely, equitable, and high-quality care, where every minute matters.

Chapter 10: Remote Care and Telemedicine

Remote care and telemedicine represent one of the most visible and transformative applications of artificial intelligence in healthcare. While telemedicine itself predates modern AI, the integration of intelligent systems has fundamentally expanded what remote care can achieve. What began as video-based consultations has evolved into a sophisticated ecosystem that includes AI-enhanced virtual visits, remote diagnostics, continuous monitoring, rehabilitation programs, and population-scale care delivery models.

The COVID-19 pandemic accelerated adoption by necessity, but the sustained growth of telemedicine reflects deeper structural changes. Healthcare systems face clinician shortages, rising chronic disease burden, geographic inequities, and growing patient expectations for convenience and continuity. AI-enhanced remote care addresses these pressures by extending clinical reach, improving efficiency, and enabling care to occur beyond traditional facilities.

This chapter examines how artificial intelligence enhances telemedicine across clinical, operational, and equity dimensions. Rather than treating telemedicine as a substitute for in-person care, AI-enabled remote care is best understood as a complementary model - one that reshapes how, when, and where healthcare is delivered.

Virtual Visits Enhanced by AI

Early telemedicine models focused primarily on synchronous video visits that attempted to replicate in-person consultations at a distance. While these visits expanded access and convenience, they often inherited many of the same limitations as traditional care, including time pressure, documentation burden, fragmented follow-up, and heavy reliance on clinician availability.

From Video Calls to Intelligent Encounters

Artificial intelligence fundamentally expands the scope of virtual visits by embedding intelligence before, during, and after the encounter, transforming telemedicine from a simple communication tool into an integrated care experience.

AI-enhanced virtual visits are best understood as intelligent clinical encounters. Rather than centering solely on real-time interaction, these encounters are supported by automated preparation, real-time decision support, and longitudinal follow-up.

This shift improves efficiency, consistency, and continuity while allowing clinicians to focus more fully on clinical reasoning and patient engagement.

Pre-Visit Intelligence and Structured Preparation

One of the most immediate benefits of AI in virtual care occurs before the clinician joins the visit. Automated intake systems use conversational interfaces to collect symptoms, medical history, medication lists, and patient-reported outcomes.

Natural language processing structures free-text responses into clinically meaningful categories and highlights key issues for review.

For example, before a virtual primary care appointment, an AI system may collect detailed symptom descriptions and duration, identify red-flag symptoms that require escalation, summarize relevant past medical history, and flag potential medication adherence issues. The system may also suggest evidence-based questions or clinical guidelines relevant to the presenting complaint.

This structured preparation reduces repetitive questioning, shortens visit duration, and improves clinical focus. Clinicians enter the encounter with a clearer understanding of the patient's concerns, enabling more efficient and meaningful interaction.

Real-Time Clinical Support During Visits

During the virtual visit itself, AI provides real-time assistance that supports clinical workflow without disrupting patient interaction. Speech recognition tools transcribe conversations automatically, reducing documentation burden and improving accuracy. AI systems can highlight key clinical concepts as they arise, suggest relevant differential diagnoses or clinical guidelines, and flag potential medication interactions based on the discussion.

In behavioral health visits, AI-driven analysis of speech patterns, such as changes in tone, pace, or affect, may support a more nuanced assessment of conditions like depression or anxiety. These insights complement, rather than replace, clinician observation and judgment.

Importantly, AI tools function strictly as decision support systems. They provide suggestions and insights, but clinicians retain full authority over interpretation, diagnosis, and treatment decisions. This preserves professional autonomy while enhancing situational awareness.

Post-Visit Follow-Up and Longitudinal Continuity

The value of AI-enhanced virtual visits extends beyond the encounter itself. After the visit, AI systems generate structured visit summaries, reinforce care instructions, schedule follow-up tests or appointments, and initiate remote monitoring or educational programs when appropriate.

Automated check-ins assess symptom progression, treatment adherence, and emerging concerns, ensuring that care continues between visits. For patients with chronic conditions, these follow-ups support early intervention and reduce the risk of deterioration.

Redefining Virtual Care

By embedding intelligence across the entire visit lifecycle, AI transforms virtual care from isolated interactions into continuous, coordinated care pathways. When implemented thoughtfully, AI-enhanced virtual visits improve efficiency, consistency, and patient experience, without diminishing the central role of human clinical judgment.

Remote Diagnostics and Monitoring

One of the most significant advances enabled by telemedicine is the extension of diagnostic capability beyond traditional clinical settings into patients' homes and everyday environments. AI-enabled remote diagnostics combine connected medical devices, mobile applications, and intelligent interpretation to approximate key elements of in-person assessment.

This shift is particularly valuable when access to clinics is limited by geography, mobility constraints, workforce shortages, or public health emergencies.

Extending Diagnostic Capability Beyond Traditional Clinics

Remote diagnostic tools span a wide range of clinical domains. Examples include AI-assisted interpretation of home electrocardiograms for cardiac rhythm assessment, smartphone-based dermatology applications that analyze images of skin lesions, remote otoscopy and digital stethoscopes that enable clinicians to examine ears and heart sounds remotely, and AI-supported home spirometry for monitoring respiratory conditions such as asthma or chronic obstructive pulmonary disease.

While these tools do not replace comprehensive in-clinic diagnostics, they enable earlier assessment, triage, and decision-making, often determining whether urgent in-person evaluation is required.

Early Detection and Risk Stratification at Home

The clinical value of remote diagnostics lies not only in convenience but also in the ability to detect early signals that might otherwise go unnoticed.

AI systems analyze data captured by home devices to identify patterns suggestive of emerging disease or worsening control. For example, subtle irregularities in home ECG recordings may prompt earlier cardiology review, while changes in spirometry trends may signal declining respiratory function before symptoms become severe.

By shifting diagnostic insight upstream, AI-enabled remote diagnostics support preventive care and reduce unnecessary emergency visits. Patients receive guidance earlier, and clinicians gain actionable information without requiring immediate in-person encounters.

Continuous Monitoring as Diagnostic Context

Remote monitoring further enhances diagnostic accuracy by providing longitudinal context rather than isolated measurements. Traditional clinical assessments often rely on single-point data collected during office visits, which may not reflect real-world variability. In contrast, continuous or frequent home monitoring captures trends over time, offering a more representative view of health status.

AI systems excel at interpreting these longitudinal data streams. In hypertension management, for example, AI analyzes home blood pressure patterns across days or weeks rather than reacting to individual readings influenced by stress or measurement conditions. In heart failure care, changes in activity levels, resting heart rate, sleep patterns, and weight collectively inform early intervention. In diabetes management, glucose variability and nocturnal trends provide more predictive insight than average glucose values alone.

By focusing on patterns rather than thresholds, AI enhances diagnostic sensitivity while reducing false alarms and unnecessary escalation.

Clinical Integration and Oversight

For remote diagnostics to be clinically meaningful, they must be integrated into established workflows.

AI systems summarize findings, assign confidence levels, and recommend potential next steps, but clinicians remain responsible for validation, interpretation, and action. Clear protocols define when remote findings warrant in-person evaluation, imaging, or specialist referral.

This integration ensures that remote diagnostics complement rather than fragment care. When supported by thoughtful governance and clinical oversight, AI-enabled remote diagnostics and monitoring expand diagnostic reach, improve early detection, and support more responsive, patient-centered telemedicine models.

Access and Equity in Rural and Underserved Areas

Rural and underserved populations face long-standing barriers to accessing timely, high-quality healthcare. These challenges include shortages of primary care clinicians and specialists, long travel distances to healthcare facilities, limited transportation options, and fewer diagnostic and treatment resources.

Geographic and Structural Barriers to Care

Specialty services such as cardiology, dermatology, oncology, and mental health care are often concentrated in urban centers, creating significant disparities in diagnosis and treatment.

Telemedicine has the potential to reduce these inequities by removing geographic constraints. However, access alone does not guarantee equity. Without thoughtful design and adequate infrastructure, telemedicine can inadvertently reinforce existing disparities.

Artificial intelligence enhances telemedicine's equity potential by enabling scalable support, flexible care models, and adaptive interfaces that better meet the needs of diverse populations.

AI-Enabled Models for Scalable and Asynchronous Care

AI plays a critical role in making telemedicine scalable in settings with limited clinical workforce capacity. Asynchronous care models, where patients and clinicians interact without requiring real-time availability, allow clinicians to manage larger patient populations more efficiently.

AI supports these models by collecting structured information, prioritizing cases, and highlighting those that require urgent attention.

Decision support tools powered by AI assist non-specialist providers in rural clinics by offering evidence-based guidance typically available only through specialist consultation. For example, AI-assisted dermatology tools analyze images of skin lesions and flag those requiring urgent evaluation, allowing primary care clinicians to triage effectively without on-site dermatologists.

Similarly, AI-supported radiology interpretation can assist in identifying abnormalities on imaging studies when specialist review is delayed.

AI as a Force Multiplier in Community Health Settings

In community health centers and outreach programs, AI-enabled virtual assistants extend the reach of limited staff. These systems provide health education, symptom triage, appointment reminders, and follow-up support in local languages, reducing reliance on overburdened clinicians and administrative personnel.

By maintaining ongoing contact between visits, virtual assistants help prevent care gaps that disproportionately affect underserved populations.

For example, AI-driven platforms may support maternal health programs in rural regions by monitoring symptoms, reinforcing prenatal care guidance, and prompting timely referrals when risk indicators emerge. In chronic disease programs, AI helps track adherence and symptoms, enabling earlier intervention despite limited in-person resources.

Addressing Digital Divide Risks

Equity is not an automatic outcome of technology adoption. Limited internet access, device availability, and digital literacy remain significant barriers in many underserved communities. To avoid exacerbating disparities, AI-enabled telemedicine systems must be designed for inclusivity.

Key design considerations include support for low-bandwidth environments, mobile-first access compatible with basic smartphones, voice-based interaction for individuals with limited literacy, and offline data capture with delayed synchronization.

These features ensure that care delivery is not restricted to populations with high-speed internet or advanced devices.

The Role of Policy and Inclusive Design

Technology alone cannot solve inequity. Public policy, infrastructure investment, and inclusive design practices are essential to realizing the equity potential of AI-enabled telemedicine. Investments in broadband access, digital literacy programs, and community-based implementation are critical complements to technological innovation.

When thoughtfully designed and supported, AI-enhanced telemedicine can reduce geographic disparities, extend specialist expertise, and promote more equitable access to care. Without such safeguards, however, it risks reinforcing the very inequities it seeks to address.

Tele-Rehabilitation and Chronic Care Programs

Tele-rehabilitation represents a fundamental shift in how rehabilitative care is delivered. Historically, physical, occupational, and speech therapy required repeated in-person visits to specialized facilities, creating barriers for patients with mobility limitations, transportation challenges, or geographic constraints. Tele-rehabilitation extends these services into the home, enabling patients to engage in therapy within their daily environments.

Rehabilitation Beyond Traditional Facilities

Artificial intelligence significantly enhances tele-rehabilitation by providing real-time assessment, feedback, and personalization. Computer vision systems analyze patient movements through smartphone cameras or connected sensors, evaluating range of motion, posture, balance, and movement symmetry.

Rather than simply counting repetitions, AI assesses movement quality, identifying compensatory patterns or incorrect techniques that may hinder recovery or increase injury risk. Patients receive immediate, actionable feedback, such as prompts to adjust posture or slow movement, without requiring constant clinician supervision.

Real-Time Feedback and Adherence Monitoring

One of the persistent challenges in rehabilitation is adherence. Patients may perform exercises incorrectly, inconsistently, or abandon programs altogether once direct supervision decreases. AI-powered tele-rehabilitation platforms address this challenge by tracking adherence objectively and providing encouragement and reminders.

For example, an AI system may detect missed sessions or declining performance and respond with motivational prompts, simplified exercises, or alerts to care teams. This closed-loop feedback improves engagement while allowing therapists to focus their time on patients who need additional support.

Personalized Recovery Pathways

AI enables rehabilitation programs to adapt dynamically to each patient's progress, pain levels, and functional goals. Rather than following rigid, time-based protocols, AI-driven systems adjust exercise selection, intensity, and progression based on objective performance data.

Post-stroke patients, for instance, may receive increasingly complex motor tasks as mobility and coordination improve. Orthopedic patients recovering from joint replacement can progress through rehabilitation phases based on movement quality and stability rather than arbitrary timelines. In pulmonary rehabilitation, AI systems adjust exercise intensity based on real-time tolerance, oxygen saturation, and symptom reporting, ensuring safety while encouraging gradual improvement.

This personalization supports more efficient recovery and reduces the risk of overexertion or delayed progress.

Chronic Care Programs Beyond Rehabilitation

Tele-rehabilitation platforms increasingly overlap with broader chronic disease management programs.

Many chronic conditions, such as diabetes, chronic obstructive pulmonary disease, heart failure, arthritis, and neurological disorders, require ongoing functional support, education, and behavioral modification rather than short-term intervention.

AI-powered telemedicine platforms integrate rehabilitation exercises with remote monitoring, education, and coaching. Patients may engage in guided activity programs, symptom tracking, and lifestyle interventions supported by virtual visits and automated check-ins. Care teams use clinician dashboards to monitor trends, identify early deterioration, and coordinate multidisciplinary support involving physicians, therapists, nurses, and health coaches.

Scalability and Health System Impact

From a health system perspective, tele-rehabilitation and AI-enabled chronic care programs support scalability and sustainability. By reducing dependence on facility-based visits, these programs lower costs, improve access, and free clinical capacity. Patients benefit from continuity, reduced fragmentation, and care that aligns more closely with real-world function.

When designed with clinical oversight, evidence-based protocols, and patient-centered engagement, AI-enhanced tele-rehabilitation becomes not merely a substitute for in-person care, but a more adaptive and accessible model for long-term recovery and chronic disease management.

Reimbursement, Standards of Care, and Sustainability

Reimbursement has historically been one of the most significant barriers to widespread telemedicine adoption.

Prior to the COVID-19 pandemic, coverage for virtual services was limited, fragmented, and often restricted to narrow use cases. Temporary policy changes during the pandemic dramatically expanded reimbursement for telehealth, remote monitoring, and virtual consultations, demonstrating that large-scale remote care delivery was both feasible and valuable.

Evolving Reimbursement Models for Remote Care

Sustaining AI-enabled remote care beyond emergency measures requires stable and clearly defined reimbursement frameworks. These frameworks must recognize forms of care that do not fit traditional, visit-based models, including asynchronous communication, continuous remote monitoring, AI-assisted triage, and team-based virtual care involving nurses, therapists, and care coordinators.

Without appropriate reimbursement, health systems may struggle to justify long-term investment in these capabilities despite demonstrated clinical benefit.

Value-based care models align more naturally with AI-enabled telemedicine. Rather than reimbursing based on visit volume, value-based arrangements reward improved outcomes, reduced hospitalizations, and better chronic disease control.

Remote monitoring programs that prevent exacerbations or reduce emergency visits directly support these goals, making sustainability more achievable when incentives are aligned with outcomes rather than encounters.

Defining Standards of Care in Virtual Settings

As telemedicine becomes a routine mode of care delivery, maintaining consistent standards of care is essential. AI-enabled virtual services must meet the same clinical, ethical, and professional standards as in-person care. This requires evolving clinical guidelines that clarify when virtual care is appropriate, when escalation to in-person evaluation is necessary, and how AI-generated insights should be documented and acted upon.

Key considerations include defining appropriate clinical indications for virtual visits, establishing expectations for documentation of AI-assisted recommendations, and ensuring that the limitations of remote assessment are clearly communicated to patients.

For example, clinicians must document when a diagnosis is provisional due to a lack of physical examination and outline follow-up plans accordingly. Continuity of care - through timely follow-up, referrals, or monitoring - must be explicitly addressed in virtual care pathways.

Ensuring Quality, Safety, and Accountability

AI-enabled telemedicine introduces new layers of complexity in accountability and oversight.

While AI systems may generate recommendations or insights, clinicians remain responsible for clinical decisions. Clear delineation of roles is critical to prevent over-reliance on automated outputs or diffusion of responsibility.

Health systems must establish governance structures that define acceptable use, validation requirements, and escalation protocols for AI tools. Documentation and audit trails are essential to support transparency, quality assurance, and post-event review. These mechanisms also protect clinicians and organizations by providing evidence of appropriate decision-making and oversight.

Regulatory and Ethical Oversight

Remote care raises important regulatory and ethical considerations, including licensure across jurisdictions, malpractice liability, and data governance. AI systems must comply with privacy and security regulations, protect patient confidentiality, and ensure informed consent regarding data use.

Transparency about how AI tools function and their limitations is central to maintaining patient trust.

Building Sustainable Remote Care Models

Long-term sustainability of AI-enabled telemedicine depends on the convergence of reimbursement reform, clear standards of care, and robust governance. When financial incentives, clinical guidelines, and ethical oversight are aligned, remote care can move from a temporary solution to a durable, integral component of modern healthcare delivery.

Conclusion

AI-enhanced telemedicine is not merely a convenience. It represents a fundamental shift in healthcare delivery. By extending care into homes, communities, and daily life, remote care models address structural limitations of traditional systems.

When thoughtfully designed and ethically governed, AI-enabled remote care improves access, continuity, efficiency, and patient experience. It does not replace in-person care, but complements it, allowing healthcare systems to deliver the right care, at the right time, in the right place.

The future of healthcare will not be confined to hospitals or clinics. It will be distributed, data-driven, and increasingly intelligent. Remote care, powered by AI, is central to that transformation.

Chapter 11: Personalized Treatment Planning

Personalized treatment planning represents one of the most clinically meaningful promises of artificial intelligence in healthcare. For much of modern medicine, treatment decisions have been guided by population-level evidence, clinical guidelines, and standardized care pathways.

While these approaches have improved outcomes overall, they often fail to account for the profound variability among individuals, including variability in biology, behavior, environment, comorbidities, and response to therapy.

Artificial intelligence enables a shift from "average patient" medicine to individualized care strategies.

By integrating diverse data sources and modeling complex interactions, AI systems support treatment plans that are tailored to an individual's risk profile, predicted response, and evolving health status. Rather than replacing clinical judgment, AI augments it, helping clinicians navigate complexity, uncertainty, and trade-offs that are increasingly difficult to manage without computational support.

This chapter explores how AI supports personalized treatment planning across the full care continuum: from risk stratification and pharmacogenomics to treatment simulation, multimorbidity management, and adaptive care pathways over time.

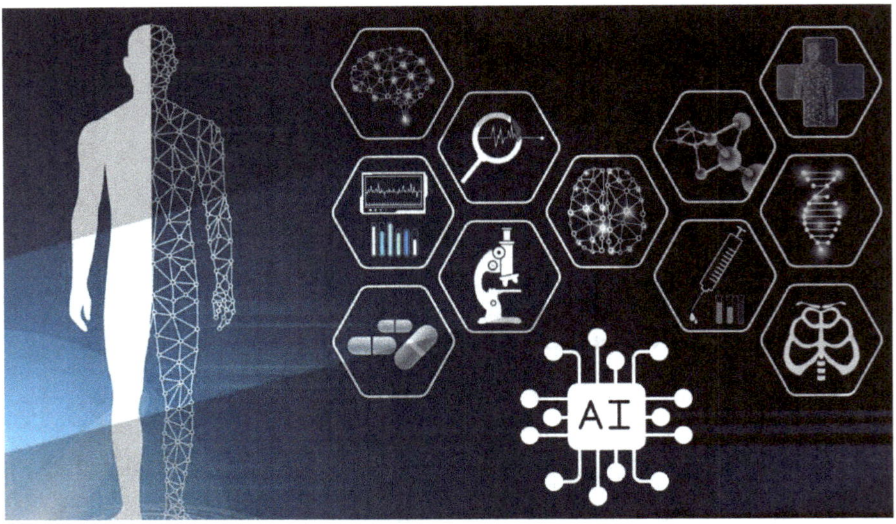

Stratifying Patients by Risk and Response

Traditional treatment guidelines are grounded in evidence generated from large clinical trials and population-level studies. While these guidelines provide an essential foundation for safe and effective care, they often obscure the substantial heterogeneity that exists between individual patients.

From One Size Fits All to Risk-Aware Care

Two people with the same diagnosis may differ widely in disease severity, progression risk, treatment tolerance, and likelihood of benefit. As a result, standardized approaches can lead to overtreatment in some patients and undertreatment in others.

AI-driven patient stratification addresses this limitation by shifting care from a one size fits all model toward a risk-aware, individualized approach.

By analyzing complex, high-dimensional datasets, AI systems identify patterns and interactions that are difficult for humans or traditional statistical models to capture. These systems recognize that risk and response emerge from combinations of clinical, biological, behavioral, and social factors rather than isolated variables.

Predictive Risk Stratification Across Clinical Domains

Predictive risk stratification uses AI models to estimate the likelihood of adverse outcomes over defined time horizons. These models integrate diverse data sources, including clinical history, laboratory results, imaging findings, genomics, lifestyle behaviors, and social determinants of health.

In cardiovascular disease, for example, AI systems predict short- and long-term risk of myocardial infarction or stroke by combining lipid profiles, blood pressure trends, cardiac imaging, genetic risk scores, medication adherence, and physical activity patterns.

This multidimensional approach provides a more precise assessment than traditional risk calculators, enabling earlier and more targeted prevention strategies.

In oncology, AI models stratify patients by likelihood of recurrence or progression based on tumor histology, molecular markers, treatment history, and response patterns. These insights inform surveillance intensity, adjuvant therapy decisions, and follow-up planning.

In surgical care, AI-driven risk models estimate the probability of complications such as infection, readmission, or prolonged recovery, supporting decisions around prehabilitation, perioperative monitoring, and discharge planning.

By aligning treatment intensity with individualized risk, clinicians can allocate resources more effectively while minimizing unnecessary interventions.

Predicting Treatment Response and Benefit

Beyond estimating risk, AI systems increasingly focus on predicting how individual patients are likely to respond to specific therapies. This capability is especially valuable in conditions with multiple treatment options that demonstrate similar average efficacy at the population level but differ substantially in individual response and side-effect profiles.

In mental health care, AI models analyze symptom clusters, prior medication responses, sleep patterns, and behavioral data to predict which antidepressant classes are most likely to be effective for a given patient. In inflammatory and autoimmune diseases, models estimate response to biologic therapies based on biomarker profiles, disease phenotype, and prior treatment history, reducing trial-and-error prescribing.

In oncology, AI-driven response prediction helps identify patients most likely to benefit from chemotherapy, immunotherapy, or targeted agents, while sparing others from unnecessary toxicity. These insights do not replace clinical judgment but provide an additional evidence layer to guide therapy selection.

Supporting Shared Decision-Making

Risk and response stratification enhances shared decision-making by making uncertainty more transparent. When clinicians can discuss individualized risk estimates and likely benefits, patients are better equipped to weigh trade-offs in the context of their values and preferences.

Ultimately, AI-driven stratification supports more precise, equitable, and patient-centered care, matching the right intervention to the right patient at the right time.

AI for Pharmacogenomics and Precision Medicine

Pharmacogenomics examines how genetic variation influences an individual's response to medications, including differences in drug metabolism, efficacy, and risk of adverse effects.

Although the principles of pharmacogenomics have been recognized for decades, clinical adoption was historically limited by the complexity of genomic data and the difficulty of translating genetic insights into actionable decisions.

Artificial intelligence has significantly accelerated this translation by enabling large-scale analysis of genomic datasets in combination with clinical outcomes.

Understanding Biological Variability in Drug Response

Genetic differences can affect how drugs are absorbed, metabolized, distributed, and eliminated.

Variants in genes encoding drug-metabolizing enzymes, transporters, or drug targets can result in under-treatment, toxicity, or unpredictable responses. AI systems excel at identifying complex patterns linking specific genetic variants to real-world treatment outcomes, helping clinicians move beyond generalized dosing recommendations toward individualized prescribing.

Optimizing Drug Selection Through AI-Driven Insights

AI-powered pharmacogenomic models support more precise drug selection by predicting which medications are most likely to be effective and safe for a given patient. These models integrate genetic data with clinical variables such as age, comorbidities, organ function, and concurrent medications.

In cardiology, for example, genetic variants affecting enzymes involved in anticoagulant metabolism can significantly influence bleeding risk. AI models combine pharmacogenomic data with clinical risk factors to recommend safer initial dosing and monitoring strategies. In oncology, AI systems analyze tumor genomic profiles to match patients with targeted therapies or immunotherapies most likely to be effective, while also identifying potential resistance mechanisms.

In psychiatry, pharmacogenomic tools supported by AI help reduce the trial-and-error approach that often characterizes antidepressant prescribing. By predicting medication tolerance and likelihood of response, these systems shorten time to effective treatment and reduce adverse effects that contribute to poor adherence.

Individualized Dosing and Toxicity Prevention

Beyond drug selection, AI enables more precise dosing strategies tailored to individual metabolic capacity.

Traditional dosing guidelines are often based on average population characteristics, whereas AI-driven models account for genetic metabolism rates, drug interactions, and physiological factors to recommend personalized dosing regimens.

For example, patients with reduced metabolic enzyme activity may require lower doses to avoid toxicity, while others may need higher doses to achieve a therapeutic effect. AI systems continuously refine dosing recommendations as new data becomes available, supporting safer long-term medication management.

Precision Medicine Beyond Genomics

While genomics is a cornerstone of precision medicine, biological variability extends beyond DNA. Precision medicine increasingly incorporates proteomics, metabolomics, microbiome composition, immune profiles, and environmental exposures. Each layer provides additional insight into disease mechanisms and treatment response.

AI systems integrate these diverse data types to create comprehensive biological profiles that inform treatment planning.

For instance, microbiome composition may influence response to immunotherapy, while metabolic profiles may affect drug efficacy and toxicity. AI's ability to manage this complexity at scale enables clinicians to move beyond disease labels toward biologically defined subtypes.From Population Averages to Individualized Care

By combining pharmacogenomics with broader precision medicine data, AI supports a fundamental shift in healthcare - from treating disease categories to treating individuals. This approach improves outcomes, reduces adverse events, and aligns care more closely with each patient's unique biological profile, marking a critical step toward truly personalized medicine.

Treatment Simulation and Optimization

One of the most transformative capabilities of artificial intelligence in personalized treatment planning is treatment simulation - the ability to model how different clinical decisions are likely to affect outcomes before those decisions are implemented. Rather than relying solely on population averages or clinician experience, AI systems use predictive modeling to explore multiple treatment scenarios in a risk-free, virtual environment.

These simulations are built on a combination of patient-specific characteristics, historical treatment-response data, disease progression models, and real-world evidence drawn from similar patients.

By integrating these inputs, AI systems estimate how an individual patient might respond to different interventions over time. This allows clinicians to anticipate benefits, risks, and downstream consequences before committing to a particular strategy.

For example, in cardiovascular care, AI models can simulate how different combinations of antihypertensive medications might affect blood pressure control, kidney function, and cardiovascular risk over several years. In oncology, simulations may estimate tumor response, toxicity burden, and survival outcomes under different treatment regimens.

These insights support more deliberate and evidence-informed decision-making.

Optimizing Treatment Sequences and Timing

Many medical conditions require sequential or combination therapies, where outcomes depend not only on which treatment is used, but also on timing, order, and duration. Traditional guidelines often recommend stepwise escalation, but these pathways may not be optimal for every patient.

AI systems excel at evaluating complex sequences. In cancer care, for instance, AI models can simulate different chemotherapy or immunotherapy sequences to balance tumor control against cumulative toxicity. In diabetes management, models evaluate medication escalation pathways, such as when to add insulin or newer agents, based on predicted glycemic response, weight impact, hypoglycemia risk, and likelihood of adherence.

In rehabilitation and chronic pain management, AI can optimize exercise or therapy progression by adjusting intensity and duration based on predicted recovery trajectories. This helps avoid both under-treatment, which delays recovery, and over-treatment, which increases the risk of injury.

Balancing Competing Clinical Objectives

Clinical decision-making often involves competing objectives. Improving symptom control may increase the risk of side effects. Aggressive treatment may improve short-term outcomes while compromising long-term quality of life. These trade-offs are frequently implicit and difficult to quantify.

AI-driven treatment simulation makes these trade-offs explicit. By presenting predicted outcomes across multiple dimensions, such as symptom relief, adverse events, functional status, and long-term risk, AI systems help clinicians and patients understand the consequences of different choices. This quantitative framing supports more transparent and patient-centered discussions.

For example, a patient with an autoimmune disease may compare a highly effective biologic therapy with a higher infection risk against a less potent option with a more favorable safety profile. AI simulations can illustrate likely scenarios under each option, supporting shared decision-making aligned with patient values.

Supporting, Not Replacing, Clinical Judgment

Importantly, treatment simulation does not eliminate uncertainty or replace clinical expertise. Models are based on available data and assumptions that may not fully capture individual complexity. Clinicians must critically interpret AI-generated projections, considering contextual factors, patient preferences, and evolving clinical information.

When used appropriately, AI-driven treatment simulation enhances - not overrides - clinical judgment. It provides a structured way to explore options, anticipate consequences, and optimize care plans in an increasingly complex therapeutic landscape.

Decision Support for Multimorbidity

Multimorbidity - the coexistence of two or more chronic conditions in the same individual - has become the norm rather than the exception, particularly among older adults.

Patients may simultaneously manage diabetes, cardiovascular disease, chronic kidney disease, arthritis, depression, or respiratory illness. While each condition has well-established clinical guidelines, those guidelines are typically developed in isolation. When applied together, they may conflict, overlap, or impose an unsustainable treatment burden.

This complexity challenges traditional clinical decision-making. Clinicians must balance competing priorities, reconcile contradictory recommendations, and consider how treatments for one condition may worsen another. Artificial intelligence offers a way to navigate this complexity by modeling interactions across diseases, treatments, and patient-specific risks.

AI as an Integrative Decision Support Layer

AI-driven decision support systems are uniquely suited to multimorbidity because they can process large numbers of variables simultaneously and evaluate nonlinear interactions. Rather than optimizing care for a single disease, these systems focus on whole-patient optimization.

AI models analyze comprehensive patient data, including diagnoses, laboratory values, medications, functional status, and social context. By integrating this information, AI systems identify how conditions interact over time and how treatment decisions affect overall health, rather than relying on isolated disease metrics.

For example, an AI system may recognize that aggressive glucose lowering in a patient with diabetes and advanced kidney disease increases the risk of hypoglycemia and hospitalization, prompting a recommendation for more conservative targets aligned with overall risk.

Managing Drug Interactions and Competing Priorities

One of the most pressing challenges in multimorbidity is managing medication interactions and cumulative risk. AI-driven decision support systems evaluate drug-drug interactions, drug-disease interactions, and additive side effects that may not be apparent when medications are considered individually.

In a patient with diabetes, heart failure, and chronic kidney disease, certain medications may benefit one condition while worsening another. AI systems can simulate different medication combinations to identify regimens that maximize overall benefit while minimizing harm. Rather than optimizing a single laboratory value, the system considers outcomes such as hospitalization risk, renal decline, cardiovascular events, and quality of life.

AI also helps prioritize clinical goals. For some patients, symptom control and functional independence may outweigh aggressive disease modification. For others, preventing long-term complications may take precedence. Decision support tools surface these trade-offs explicitly, supporting more individualized care planning.

Reducing Treatment Burden and Polypharmacy

Multimorbidity often results in polypharmacy, with patients taking numerous medications with complex dosing schedules. This increases the risk of adverse events, reduces adherence, and contributes to patient fatigue and disengagement.

AI systems support treatment simplification by identifying redundant therapies, low-value interventions, and opportunities to consolidate care plans. For example, an AI model may suggest discontinuing a marginally beneficial medication that adds side-effect risk without meaningful improvement in outcomes or recommend a single agent that addresses multiple conditions.

Reducing treatment burden is not merely a convenience as it directly improves safety, adherence, and quality of life - outcomes that are often underemphasized in disease-specific guidelines.

Supporting Shared and Goal-Oriented Care

Ultimately, AI-driven decision support for multimorbidity enables more goal-oriented, patient-centered care. By integrating complex information and presenting clear, prioritized options, AI helps clinicians and patients make decisions aligned with individual values, capacities, and life circumstances.

Rather than forcing patients to fit guidelines, AI helps adapt care to the patient - an essential shift in an era where multimorbidity is the rule, not the exception.

Adaptive Care Pathways Over Time

Healthcare is not a single decision or intervention, but a continuous process that unfolds over time. Patients' health status, risks, preferences, and life circumstances evolve, often in ways that are unpredictable. A treatment plan that is optimal today may become ineffective, burdensome, or misaligned with patient goals months or years later.

Healthcare as a Dynamic, Evolving Process

Traditional care models, which rely on periodic reassessment during scheduled visits, often struggle to keep pace with this dynamic reality.

Artificial intelligence enables adaptive care pathways - care plans that evolve continuously in response to changing data rather than remaining fixed until the next clinical encounter. This approach reframes care planning as an ongoing, responsive process rather than a series of static decisions.

Continuous Learning From Longitudinal Patient Data

At the core of adaptive care pathways is continuous learning. AI systems update predictions and recommendations as new data becomes available, integrating clinical measurements, laboratory results, treatment responses, adherence patterns, lifestyle changes, and patient-reported outcomes.

Instead of reassessing risk or effectiveness at discrete intervals, AI models refine their understanding of each patient in near real time.

For example, in diabetes management, an AI system may adjust treatment recommendations as glucose trends, activity levels, or dietary patterns change. If adherence declines or variability increases, the system may prompt reassessment, suggest alternative therapies, or intensify education and support.

Similarly, in cardiovascular disease, evolving blood pressure patterns or symptom reports may trigger earlier medication adjustment or monitoring.

This continuous recalibration keeps care plans aligned with the patient's current needs rather than outdated assumptions.

Anticipating Change Rather Than Reacting to Crisis

Adaptive care pathways also shift healthcare from reactive to anticipatory. By modeling disease trajectories, AI systems can forecast likely future needs and prompt timely intervention. This proactive approach reduces the likelihood of crisis-driven care and supports smoother transitions across disease stages.

In chronic pain management, for instance, AI may recognize diminishing response to a particular therapy and recommend alternative modalities before functional decline occurs. In oncology survivorship, care pathways may gradually shift from active treatment to long-term monitoring, rehabilitation, and prevention as recurrence risk decreases. In preventive care, interventions may intensify when risk rises and relax when stability is sustained, avoiding unnecessary treatment burden.

Supporting Long-Term Engagement and Adherence

Sustained engagement is essential for long-term outcomes, particularly in chronic disease management. Adaptive pathways support engagement by adjusting treatment intensity, goals, and communication strategies over time. Rather than delivering repetitive or irrelevant interventions, AI systems tailor recommendations to the patient's current context.

For example, a patient early in a lifestyle modification program may receive frequent coaching and reminders, while a stable, adherent patient may receive less intensive support. When engagement declines, the system can prompt reassessment or escalation, ensuring that support is responsive rather than rigid.

Aligning Care With Evolving Patient Goals

Crucially, adaptation is not limited to clinical metrics. Patient preferences, values, and goals evolve over time, and AI-enabled care pathways can incorporate these changes explicitly. Patient-reported goals, such as maintaining independence, reducing symptom burden, or prioritizing quality of life, can be integrated alongside clinical data.

By continuously aligning care with what matters most to the individual, adaptive pathways support truly personalized medicine. AI does not replace the clinician–patient relationship, but strengthens it by ensuring that care remains responsive, relevant, and aligned throughout the patient's journey.

Conclusion

Personalized treatment planning is where artificial intelligence delivers some of its most tangible clinical value. By integrating risk stratification, biological insights, simulation, multimorbidity management, and adaptive pathways, AI supports more precise, responsive, and humane care.

This transformation does not eliminate uncertainty or replace clinicians. Instead, it equips healthcare professionals with tools to navigate complexity thoughtfully and transparently. When used responsibly, AI enables medicine to move beyond standardized protocols toward care that recognizes each patient as biologically unique and dynamically evolving.

Personalized treatment planning is not a future aspiration - it is an emerging reality. Artificial intelligence is making individualized care scalable, evidence-informed, and sustainable in healthcare systems that increasingly demand all three.

Part III

Enablers and Challenges

Chapter 12: Data Governance, Privacy, and Security

Artificial intelligence in healthcare is fundamentally dependent on data. Every predictive model, decision support system, and personalized care pathway relies on access to large volumes of health information, such as clinical records, images, genomic data, sensor streams, and patient-reported outcomes.

While this data enables powerful insights, it also introduces significant ethical, legal, and operational responsibilities.

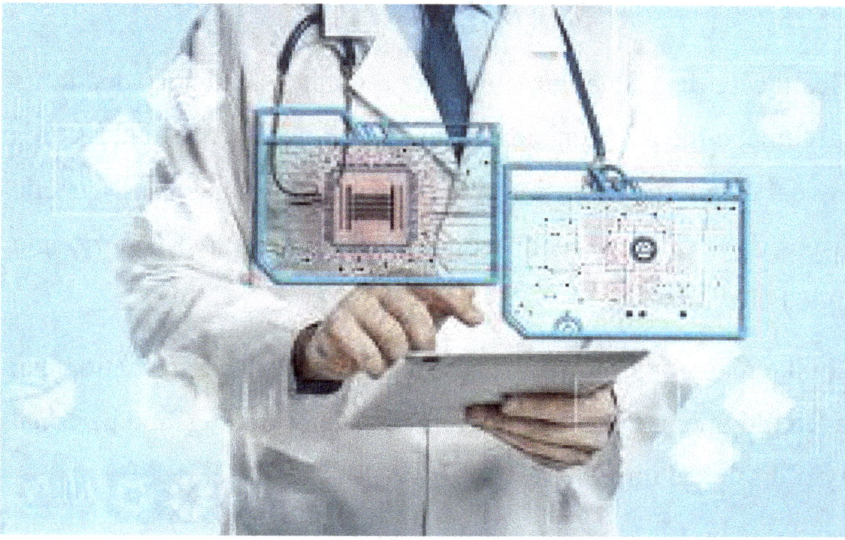

Unlike many other industries, healthcare data is deeply personal, highly sensitive, and tightly regulated. Errors in data governance can lead not only to technical failures but also to violations of privacy, loss of patient trust, regulatory penalties, and real-world harm.

As AI systems become more embedded in healthcare delivery, robust data governance, privacy protection, and security practices are no longer optional - they are foundational requirements.

This chapter examines how healthcare organizations can responsibly manage data used in AI systems. It explores regulatory frameworks, consent and de-identification practices, cybersecurity risks, and interoperability standards, emphasizing that trustworthy AI depends as much on governance as on algorithms.

Healthcare Data Regulations

Healthcare data falls into a distinct regulatory category due to its sensitivity and the potential consequences of misuse. Medical records can reveal deeply personal information, including diagnoses, genetic predispositions, mental health conditions, reproductive history, and lifestyle behaviors.

Unlike many other forms of personal data, health information can affect employment, insurance eligibility, social standing, and personal safety if disclosed improperly.

Because of these risks, healthcare data is governed by some of the most stringent regulatory frameworks worldwide. These regulations are designed to protect patient autonomy, preserve trust in healthcare systems, ensure data accuracy, and establish clear accountability when data is used for clinical care, research, public health, or artificial intelligence development.

As AI increasingly relies on large-scale health data, regulatory oversight has become even more critical.

Core Principles Underlying Health Data Regulation

Although healthcare data regulations vary by country, most are built around shared principles. These include informed consent for data use, purpose limitation to ensure data is used only for defined objectives, data minimization to reduce unnecessary exposure, strong security safeguards, and transparency regarding how data is processed.

Many frameworks also emphasize patient rights, such as access to records, correction of inaccuracies, and, in some jurisdictions, the right to data portability or deletion.

These principles shape how health data can be collected, shared, and analyzed, particularly when used to train or deploy AI systems.

Major Regulatory Frameworks Across Jurisdictions

Several major regulatory regimes define healthcare data governance globally.

In the United States, the Health Insurance Portability and Accountability Act (HIPAA) governs the use, disclosure, and protection of protected health information by covered entities and their business associates. HIPAA establishes standards for privacy, security, and breach notification, forming the backbone of U.S. health data compliance.

In the European Union, the General Data Protection Regulation (GDPR) provides a comprehensive framework for personal data protection, classifying health data as a special category requiring heightened safeguards. GDPR introduces requirements around lawful processing, explicit consent, data minimization, and individual rights, including the right to explanation in certain automated decision-making contexts.

Many countries have national data protection acts or health-specific legislation that governs medical records, secondary use of data for research, cross-border data transfer, and public health reporting. Increasingly, these laws address AI use explicitly, recognizing that automated analytics and decision support introduce novel risks beyond traditional data processing.

Regulation of AI-Enabled Data Use

Regulators are moving beyond conventional privacy protections to address how AI systems process health data and influence clinical decisions. Emerging regulatory expectations focus on transparency in automated decision-making, explainability of AI-driven outputs, accountability for algorithmic outcomes, and ongoing performance monitoring.

Some jurisdictions classify AI systems based on clinical risk, imposing stricter requirements on tools that influence diagnosis or treatment.

These developments reflect growing recognition that AI does not merely store or transmit data, but actively shapes decisions, making governance of data use inseparable from governance of AI behavior.

Operational Implications for Health Systems

For healthcare organizations, regulatory compliance is not a one-time exercise but an ongoing operational responsibility. Compliance affects how data is collected, stored, shared, and analyzed throughout the AI lifecycle. Health systems must ensure that AI development pipelines, vendor relationships, data-sharing agreements, and deployment practices align with regulatory expectations.

Meeting these requirements demands close collaboration between clinical leadership, legal and compliance teams, data scientists, and information security professionals. As AI capabilities evolve, so too must governance frameworks, ensuring that innovation proceeds without compromising patient rights, safety, or trust.

Consent, Anonymization, and De-identification

Consent is a cornerstone of ethical use of healthcare data. Patients must understand how their data is collected, used, and shared, particularly when data is used beyond direct care, such as for AI training or research.

In AI-enabled systems, consent becomes more complex. Data may be reused, combined across sources, or analyzed in ways not anticipated at the time of collection. Clear consent frameworks are essential to maintain trust and comply with regulations.

Effective consent practices include:

- Clear explanation of data use purposes
- Distinction between care delivery and secondary use
- Options to opt in or out where appropriate
- Mechanisms to withdraw consent
- Ongoing communication when data use evolves

Dynamic consent models, supported by digital platforms, allow patients to update preferences over time.

Anonymization and De-identification Techniques

To reduce privacy risk, healthcare organizations often use anonymization or de-identification when working with large datasets.

- De-identification removes or obscures direct identifiers such as names, addresses, and identification numbers.

- Anonymization aims to irreversibly prevent re-identification, even when data is combined with other sources.

AI complicates these approaches. Machine learning models can sometimes infer identity or sensitive attributes from seemingly anonymized data, particularly when datasets are rich or combined across domains.

Advanced techniques include:

- Data masking and generalization
- Differential privacy, which introduces controlled noise
- Synthetic data generation
- Federated learning, where models are trained without centralizing data

Selecting the appropriate approach depends on use case, risk tolerance, and regulatory requirements.

Balancing Utility and Privacy

There is an inherent tension between data utility and privacy protection. Excessive de-identification may degrade model performance, while insufficient safeguards increase risk.

Responsible governance requires balancing these priorities transparently and defensibly, with oversight from ethics committees and data governance bodies.

Cybersecurity in AI Systems

Artificial intelligence significantly expands the cybersecurity attack surface in healthcare.

In addition to traditional IT infrastructure such as electronic health records and hospital networks, AI introduces new components that must be protected, including data pipelines, model training environments, algorithm repositories, application programming interfaces, and cloud-based deployment platforms.

Each component represents a potential entry point for malicious actors.

Why AI Expands the Healthcare Attack Surface

Healthcare is a particularly attractive target due to the value of health data and the sector's dependence on system availability.

Cyberattacks in healthcare can have immediate clinical consequences, disrupting care delivery, delaying treatment, or compromising patient safety. Threats associated with AI systems include data breaches exposing sensitive health information, ransomware attacks that disable clinical systems, theft of proprietary models or intellectual property, data poisoning attacks that corrupt training datasets, and adversarial attacks designed to manipulate model outputs.

Unlike conventional software, AI systems can be compromised in ways that are subtle and difficult to detect. A manipulated model may continue to function while producing biased or unsafe recommendations, underscoring the need for robust cybersecurity.

Protecting Data Across the AI Lifecycle

Effective cybersecurity in AI systems requires protection across the entire lifecycle of data and models. Security considerations begin at data collection, where information is transmitted from devices, sensors, and clinical systems. Secure communication protocols, device authentication, and encryption in transit are essential to prevent interception or tampering.

During data storage, encryption at rest, strict access controls, and network segmentation help limit exposure. AI training environments require additional safeguards, including controlled access, audit logging, and validation checks to detect data poisoning or unauthorized modifications. Model repositories must be protected against theft, version tampering, or unauthorized deployment.

In deployment, secure APIs, strong authentication mechanisms, and continuous monitoring help prevent misuse or exploitation.

Zero-trust architectures - where no system or user is implicitly trusted - are increasingly adopted to minimize lateral movement within networks. Role-based access control ensures that users and systems have only the permissions necessary for their functions.

Monitoring, Detection, and Anomaly Response

Cybersecurity does not end at deployment. Continuous monitoring is essential to detect anomalies that may indicate an attack or misuse. AI systems themselves can support cybersecurity by identifying unusual access patterns, unexpected model behavior, or data drift that may signal compromise.

Healthcare organizations must establish clear escalation procedures when anomalies are detected. Rapid investigation and containment can prevent minor incidents from escalating into system-wide failures.

Importantly, cybersecurity monitoring must be integrated into clinical risk management, recognizing that technical disruptions can translate directly into patient harm.

Resilience and Incident Response Planning

Given the inevitability of cyber threats, healthcare organizations must plan for breaches as well as prevention. Comprehensive incident response plans should include rapid detection and containment procedures, continuity-of-care protocols to maintain safe operations during system outages, and clear communication pathways with regulators, partners, and patients.

Post-incident analysis is equally important. Organizations should assess root causes, remediate vulnerabilities, and update security controls to prevent recurrence. AI systems used in clinical settings should incorporate fail-safe mechanisms that limit unsafe behavior during outages or attacks, such as reverting to conservative defaults or disabling automated recommendations.

Cybersecurity as a Patient Safety Imperative

In AI-enabled healthcare, cybersecurity is inseparable from patient safety. Protecting data, models, and systems is not merely a technical obligation but a clinical one. As AI becomes more deeply embedded in care delivery, robust cybersecurity practices are essential to maintaining trust, safety, and resilience in modern health systems.

Interoperability Standards

AI systems derive value from integrating data across sources, such as electronic health records, imaging systems, laboratories, wearables, and public health databases. Without interoperability, data remains siloed, limiting insight and scalability.

Interoperability is not just a technical challenge; it is a governance and organizational one.

Standards for Data Exchange

Healthcare interoperability relies on common standards that define data structure, terminology, and exchange protocols. These standards enable AI systems to ingest data consistently and accurately.

Key elements include:

- Structured clinical data formats
- Standardized coding systems for diagnoses, procedures, and medications
- APIs that support real-time data exchange
- Metadata standards to preserve context and provenance

Consistent data representation improves model generalizability and reduces bias introduced by local documentation practices.

Interoperability and Vendor Ecosystems

AI solutions often involve multiple vendors and platforms. Interoperability standards reduce vendor lock-in and support modular system design. This flexibility allows organizations to evolve AI capabilities without wholesale system replacement.

From a governance perspective, interoperability supports transparency, auditability, and continuity across care settings.

Challenges and Trade-offs

Achieving interoperability requires investment, coordination, and compromise. Legacy systems, proprietary formats, and inconsistent data quality remain barriers. However, without interoperability, AI-driven healthcare cannot scale safely or equitably.

Conclusion

Data governance, privacy, and security are not just peripheral concerns in AI-enabled healthcare. They are central determinants of success or failure. Sophisticated algorithms cannot compensate for weak governance, insecure systems, or erosion of patient trust.

Responsible AI requires:

- Clear regulatory alignment
- Ethical consent practices
- Robust de-identification strategies
- Strong cybersecurity defenses
- Interoperable data infrastructure

When these foundations are in place, AI can be deployed confidently on a large scale. When they are neglected, even technically impressive systems risk rejection, harm, or collapse.

As healthcare increasingly relies on intelligent systems, trust becomes the most valuable asset. Data governance is how that trust is earned, protected, and sustained.

Chapter 13: Ethical, Legal, and Social Implications of Artificial Intelligence in Healthcare

Artificial intelligence has moved from experimental innovation to operational reality in healthcare. As AI systems increasingly influence diagnosis, triage, treatment planning, and system-level decision-making, they raise fundamental ethical, legal, and social questions that extend far beyond technical performance.

Unlike many other technologies, AI in healthcare directly affects human well-being, autonomy, trust, and rights. Errors, biases, or misuse can result not only in inefficiency but in real harm to patients and populations.

This chapter examines the ethical, legal, and social implications (ELSI) of AI in healthcare. It explores how algorithmic bias can undermine fairness, how accountability must be defined in AI-assisted care, how informed consent must evolve, how legal liability is reshaped, and how societal perceptions influence acceptance and legitimacy.

Together, these considerations form the foundation for responsible, trustworthy, and sustainable AI adoption in healthcare.

Bias, Fairness, and Algorithmic Transparency

Bias in healthcare AI does not arise from malicious intent but from the data, assumptions, and design choices that shape algorithms. Healthcare data reflects historical inequities in access, diagnosis, and treatment. When AI systems are trained on such data, they may reproduce or amplify these inequities.

Sources of Bias in Healthcare AI

Common sources of bias include:

- Representation bias that occurs when certain populations (such as women, ethnic minorities, rural patients, or people with disabilities) are underrepresented in training datasets.

- Measurement bias, where clinical variables are measured differently across populations, often due to access disparities or diagnostic practices.
- Label bias, where outcomes used for training reflect systemic inequities rather than true disease burden.

For example, algorithms trained on healthcare spending data may underestimate disease severity in populations that historically receive less care, leading to under-allocation of resources. Similarly, dermatology algorithms trained primarily on lighter skin tones may perform poorly in detecting conditions in darker skin.

Fairness as a Clinical and Ethical Requirement

Fairness in healthcare AI is not merely a technical goal - it is a clinical and ethical obligation. AI systems must be evaluated not only for average accuracy but for performance across subgroups defined by race, sex, age, socioeconomic status, and comorbidities.

Approaches to improving fairness include:

- Diverse and representative training datasets
- Subgroup-specific performance evaluation
- Bias auditing throughout the model lifecycle
- Adaptive models that recalibrate across populations

However, fairness often involves trade-offs. Improving performance for one group may reduce performance for another.

Ethical governance must guide these decisions transparently, prioritizing equity and patient safety.

Algorithmic Transparency and Explainability

Transparency is essential for trust in AI-assisted healthcare. Clinicians must understand why a system generates a particular recommendation, especially when it influences diagnosis or treatment.

Algorithmic transparency includes:

- Clear documentation of model purpose, data sources, and limitations
- Explainable outputs that highlight key contributing factors
- Disclosure of uncertainty and confidence levels

While some AI models (particularly deep learning systems) are inherently complex, explainability techniques, such as feature attribution, visual overlays, or rule-based summaries, can bridge the gap between performance and interpretability.

Without transparency, AI risks becoming an opaque authority rather than a clinical support tool.

Accountability and Trust

One of the most challenging ethical questions in AI-enabled healthcare is accountability. When an AI system contributes to a decision that leads to harm, responsibility cannot be attributed solely to the algorithm.

Who Is Responsible When AI Is Involved?

Accountability in AI-assisted care is shared across:

- Healthcare organizations deploying the system
- Clinicians using AI-generated insights
- Developers and vendors designing and maintaining the technology
- Regulators approving and overseeing its use

Clear accountability frameworks are essential to prevent diffusion of responsibility, where no party feels fully accountable for outcomes.

Maintaining Clinical Authority and Human Oversight

Ethical AI deployment requires that clinicians retain ultimate decision-making authority. AI systems should support and not override professional judgment.

This includes:

- The ability to question or override AI recommendations
- Training clinicians to understand system limitations
- Avoiding automation bias, where users defer excessively to AI output

Trust in AI is strongest when clinicians view it as a collaborator rather than a replacement.

Institutional Trust and Governance

Trust also operates at an institutional level. Patients and clinicians must trust that health systems deploy AI responsibly, ethically, and transparently.

Effective governance structures include:

- Multidisciplinary AI oversight committees
- Continuous performance monitoring
- Clear escalation and incident review processes
- Public communication about AI use and safeguards

Trust is not granted automatically. Rather, it is earned through accountability and demonstrated integrity.

Informed Consent for AI Use

Traditional informed consent focuses on clinical procedures or the use of data. AI introduces new complexities, including automated decision-making, the use of secondary data, and continuous learning systems.

Patients may be unaware that AI influences their care, how their data is used, or what role automation plays in decision-making.

Elements of Meaningful AI Consent

Ethically sound consent for AI use should include:

- Disclosure that AI is involved in care delivery

- Explanation of the AI system's role and limitations
- Clarification of how patient data is used and protected
- Information about human oversight and escalation pathways

Consent does not require patients to understand technical details, but it does require transparency about impact and agency.

Dynamic and Context-Sensitive Consent

Because AI systems evolve over time, consent should be viewed as an ongoing process rather than a one-time event. This is especially relevant for continuous monitoring, learning systems, and the use of secondary data.

Digital platforms can support dynamic consent, allowing patients to:

- Update preferences
- Opt in or out of specific AI-enabled services
- Receive updates about system changes

Legal Liability in AI-Enabled Care

Legal systems worldwide are grappling with how to assign liability in AI-assisted healthcare. Traditional malpractice frameworks assume human decision-makers, while AI introduces shared agency.

Key legal questions include:

- Is AI a medical device or a decision-support tool?
- How is negligence defined when AI is involved?
- Who is liable for algorithmic errors or bias?

Shared Responsibility Models

Most legal frameworks are moving toward shared responsibility rather than assigning liability to AI itself. Clinicians remain accountable for decisions, while organizations and vendors bear responsibility for system safety, validation, and transparency.

Clear documentation of AI recommendations, clinician actions, and escalation decisions is essential for legal defensibility.

Risk Management and Legal Safeguards

Healthcare organizations can mitigate legal risk through:

- Rigorous validation and documentation
- Defined scope-of-use policies
- Continuous monitoring and audit trails
- Clear clinician training and guidance

Legal clarity will continue to evolve, but proactive governance is essential.

Societal Perceptions and Patient Rights

Societal acceptance of AI in healthcare depends on trust, fairness, and perceived benefit. Public skepticism often arises from fears of dehumanization, surveillance, or loss of control.

Transparent communication about AI's role, benefits, and safeguards is essential to maintaining legitimacy.

Patient Rights in the Age of AI

AI-enabled healthcare must respect fundamental patient rights, including:

- The right to informed decision-making
- The right to privacy and data protection
- The right to explanation and appeal
- The right to equitable treatment

Patients should not be subject to purely automated decisions without human review in high-stakes contexts.

Avoiding a Two-Tiered System

There is a risk that AI could deepen disparities if advanced tools are available only to well-resourced systems or populations. Ethical deployment requires intentional efforts to ensure equitable access and benefit.

AI should be a force for inclusion, not stratification.

Conclusion

Ethical, legal, and social considerations are not barriers to AI innovation. Rather, they are prerequisites for its legitimacy and sustainability in healthcare. Without fairness, transparency, accountability, and respect for patient rights, AI risks undermining trust and exacerbating harm.

Responsible AI in healthcare demands continuous ethical reflection, interdisciplinary governance, and patient-centered design. When guided by these principles, AI can enhance, not diminish, the human values at the heart of medicine.

Chapter 14: Implementation Strategies and Change Management

The successful adoption of artificial intelligence in healthcare is not primarily a technical challenge, but an organizational one. While AI models may demonstrate impressive accuracy in controlled environments, their real-world impact depends on how effectively they are implemented, integrated, governed, and sustained within complex health systems.

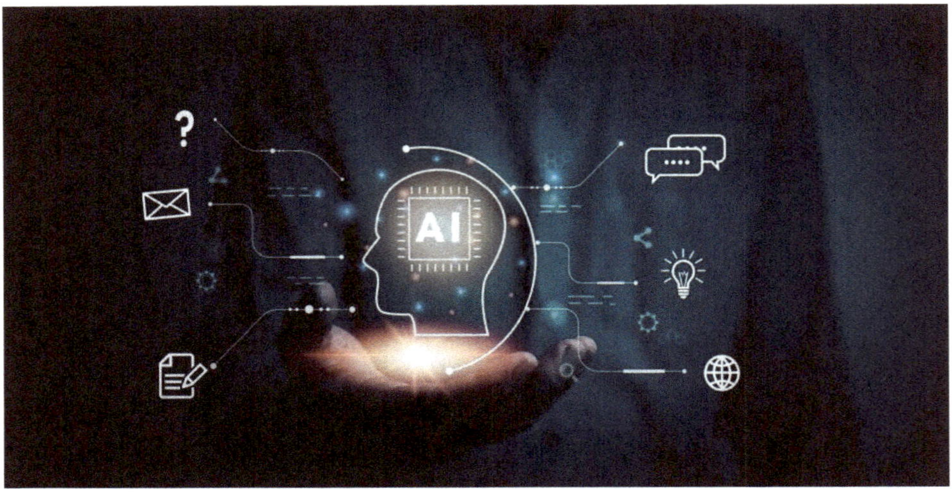

Many AI initiatives fail not because the technology is flawed, but because organizations underestimate the human, cultural, and operational changes required.

This chapter examines the practical realities of implementing AI in healthcare. It focuses on readiness assessment, workflow integration, workforce transformation, performance evaluation, and scaling across health systems.

Together, these elements form a structured approach to moving AI from pilot projects to sustainable, system-wide capability.

AI Readiness Assessments

The implementation of artificial intelligence in healthcare is not a plug-and-play exercise. Organizations that attempt to deploy AI without adequate preparation often encounter stalled pilots, clinician pushbacks, poor model performance, and erosion of trust.

Why Readiness Matters

AI readiness refers to an organization's ability to adopt, integrate, govern, and sustain AI solutions in a way that delivers measurable clinical and operational value.

Crucially, readiness is not limited to technology. While computing infrastructure and data availability are necessary, they are far from sufficient. True readiness encompasses leadership alignment, governance maturity, workforce capability, cultural openness to change, and clarity of strategic intent. A structured AI readiness assessment allows organizations to move from opportunistic experimentation toward deliberate, scalable adoption.

Rather than asking "Can we deploy AI?", readiness assessments help organizations ask the more important question: "Are we prepared to use AI responsibly and effectively?"

Core Dimensions of AI Readiness

A comprehensive AI readiness assessment typically examines several interdependent domains, each of which influences the success or failure of AI initiatives. Here are some core dimensions of readiness that must be explored while implementing AI in healthcare.

- Data Readiness

Data is the foundation of all AI systems. Healthcare organizations must assess not only whether data exists, but whether it is usable, trustworthy, and governable. Key considerations include the structure and standardization of electronic health records, completeness and longitudinal depth of data, consistency of coding practices, and the presence of robust data governance policies.

Interoperability is particularly critical. AI systems often require data from multiple sources, including clinical, operational, imaging, and patient-generated. Fragmented or siloed data environments limit model performance and scalability. Without strong data readiness, even the most advanced AI tools will produce unreliable or biased outputs.

- Technical and Architectural Readiness

AI adoption requires infrastructure that can support data ingestion, model training, deployment, and ongoing monitoring. Readiness assessments evaluate whether organizations have adequate computing capacity, secure storage, integration layers with existing clinical systems, and scalable deployment environments.

Decisions about cloud versus on-premise infrastructure, vendor platforms, and cybersecurity controls should align with long-term organizational strategy. Short-term experimentation without architectural planning often leads to technical debt and security risk.

- Governance and Leadership Alignment

AI initiatives demand strong leadership sponsorship and clear accountability. Readiness assessments examine whether executive leadership understands AI's capabilities and limitations, whether decision-making authority is clearly defined, and whether ethical, legal, and clinical oversight structures are in place.

Effective governance includes defined processes for model validation, performance monitoring, bias assessment, and escalation when risks are identified. Without leadership alignment and governance clarity, AI projects frequently stall or fail to progress beyond pilot phases.

- Workforce and Cultural Readiness

Even technically sound AI systems will fail if clinicians and staff do not trust or use them. Readiness assessments, therefore, evaluate digital literacy, familiarity with data-driven tools, prior experience with innovation, and prevailing attitudes toward automation and decision support.

Concerns about loss of autonomy, increased workload, or job displacement must be acknowledged and addressed proactively. Organizations with cultures that support learning, transparency, and collaboration are far more likely to achieve sustainable AI adoption.

From Assessment to Actionable Roadmap

The purpose of an AI readiness assessment is not to assign a maturity score or pass-fail judgment. Its value lies in informing a realistic, phased implementation roadmap. Based on assessment findings, organizations may choose to begin with low-risk, high-value use cases, invest first in data and governance foundations, or defer deployment until critical gaps are addressed.

By grounding AI strategy in readiness rather than hype, healthcare organizations can sequence adoption thoughtfully, reduce risk, and maximize long-term impact. Readiness assessments transform AI from a reactive experiment into a strategic capability - one that is built to endure.

Clinical Workflow Integration

Even highly accurate AI tools fail if they disrupt clinical workflows. Healthcare environments are time-constrained, interruption-heavy, and safety-critical. Any additional cognitive burden or inefficiency reduces adoption and increases risk.

AI must fit seamlessly into existing workflows rather than forcing clinicians to adapt to the technology.

Principles of Effective Workflow Integration

Embed AI Where Decisions Are Made

AI insights should appear within the systems clinicians already use, such as electronic health records, imaging viewers, or monitoring dashboards. Standalone interfaces requiring separate logins are rarely adopted.

For example, an AI sepsis alert should surface within the clinician's patient list or vital sign view, not in a separate application.

Timing and Relevance of Information

AI recommendations must arrive at the right moment in the care process. Alerts delivered too early, too late, or without context are ignored.

Effective systems:

- Deliver insights when action is possible
- Suppress alerts when intervention is unlikely
- Prioritize relevance over completeness

Minimize Cognitive Load

AI outputs should be concise, interpretable, and actionable. Rather than presenting raw scores, systems should answer:

- What is happening?
- Why does it matter?
- What action should be considered?

Explainability supports trust and safe decision-making.

Human-in-the-Loop Design

Workflow integration must preserve human oversight. Clinicians should:

- Understand how recommendations were generated
- Have the ability to override or ignore AI output
- Provide feedback that improves system performance

This collaborative model reinforces AI as decision support rather than automation.

Training and Workforce Transformation

AI adoption reshapes roles, responsibilities, and skill requirements across healthcare organizations. Rather than replacing clinicians, AI shifts the nature of clinical work, reducing routine tasks while increasing emphasis on judgment, interpretation, and patient communication.

Workforce transformation is therefore central to the success of implementation.

Training Clinicians to Work With AI

Clinicians do not need to become data scientists, but they must understand:

- What AI systems can and cannot do
- How to interpret outputs and uncertainty
- When to trust recommendations and when to question them
- How to communicate AI-informed decisions to patients

Training should focus on clinical relevance rather than technical depth.

New Roles and Interdisciplinary Teams

AI implementation creates new roles within healthcare organizations, including:

- Clinical informatics specialists
- AI product owners
- Data governance leads
- Model performance monitors

Interdisciplinary collaboration between clinicians, data scientists, IT teams, and compliance professionals becomes essential.

Addressing Fear and Resistance

Resistance often stems from fear of loss of autonomy or professional identity. Transparent communication is critical:

- AI augments clinical expertise rather than replacing it
- Clinicians retain decision authority
- AI reduces administrative burden and cognitive overload

Change management strategies must acknowledge emotional and professional concerns, not dismiss them.

Evaluation Metrics

Evaluating AI systems solely based on technical accuracy is inadequate. High performance in development does not guarantee clinical value or safety in deployment.

Healthcare AI must be evaluated across multiple dimensions.

Categories of Evaluation Metrics

1. Clinical Impact Metrics

- Improvement in patient outcomes
- Reduction in adverse events
- Earlier detection or intervention
- Changes in morbidity or mortality

2. Workflow and Efficiency Metrics

- Time saved per clinician
- Reduction in documentation burden
- Improved throughput or capacity
- Reduced alert fatigue

3. Adoption and Trust Metrics

- Clinician usage rates
- Override frequency
- User satisfaction
- Qualitative feedback

4. Equity and Fairness Metrics

- Performance across demographic groups
- Detection of bias or disparity
- Impact on access and outcomes

5. Safety and Risk Metrics

- False positive and false negative rates
- Near-miss events
- Escalation appropriateness

Continuous Monitoring and Recalibration

AI performance degrades over time due to changes in population, practice patterns, or data quality. Continuous monitoring is essential to detect drift and unintended consequences.

Evaluation is an ongoing process, not a one-time validation.

Scaling Solutions in Health Systems

Many organizations succeed with AI pilots but fail to scale. Common barriers include:

- Fragmented ownership
- Inconsistent governance
- Lack of standardization
- Insufficient infrastructure

Scaling requires shifting from experimentation to enterprise strategy.

Standardization and Reusability

Scalable AI programs emphasize:

- Shared data platforms
- Reusable integration components
- Consistent governance frameworks
- Common evaluation standards

This reduces duplication and accelerates deployment across departments.

Balancing Centralization and Local Adaptation

While governance and infrastructure should be centralized, clinical implementation must allow local adaptation. Different departments may require tailored workflows, thresholds, or escalation pathways.

Successful scaling balances standardization with clinical flexibility.

Sustainability and Long-Term Value

Scaling AI requires sustainable funding models, ongoing training, and performance management. Organizations must plan for:

- Model maintenance and updates
- Regulatory compliance
- Vendor management
- Workforce evolution

AI should be treated as a long-term capability, not a one-off investment.

Conclusion

AI implementation in healthcare is not a technical rollout. It is a strategic transformation. Success depends on readiness assessment, thoughtful workflow integration, workforce engagement, rigorous evaluation, and disciplined scaling.

Organizations that treat AI as a socio-technical system - one that integrates technology, people, processes, and values - are far more likely to realize its promise. Those that neglect change management risk creating sophisticated tools that fail to improve care.

The next chapter turns to regulatory frameworks and standards, examining how oversight structures shape the safe and effective deployment of AI at scale.

Chapter 15: Regulatory Frameworks and Standards

As artificial intelligence becomes increasingly embedded in healthcare delivery, regulation plays a defining role in shaping how AI systems are developed, deployed, and governed.

Unlike many digital innovations, healthcare AI operates in high-risk environments where errors can directly affect patient safety, clinical outcomes, and public trust. Regulatory frameworks and standards, therefore, serve not as obstacles to innovation but as essential safeguards that ensure AI technologies are safe, effective, ethical, and accountable.

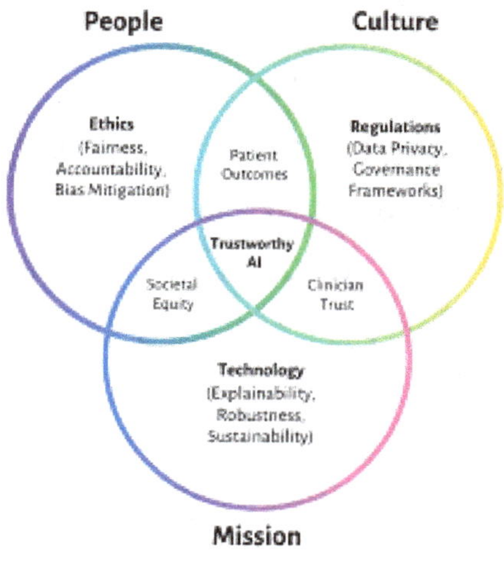

This chapter examines the global regulatory landscape for AI in healthcare. It explores the role of major regulatory bodies, the concept of Software as a Medical Device (SaMD), certification and compliance mechanisms, and ongoing efforts toward international harmonization.

Understanding these frameworks is critical for healthcare organizations, developers, and policymakers seeking to deploy AI responsibly at scale.

Regulatory Bodies and Approval Pathways

Healthcare regulation exists to protect patients, ensure the quality of care, and maintain trust in medical systems. AI introduces new regulatory challenges because it often operates as a decision-support layer rather than a traditional medical device. Algorithms may evolve over time, learn from new data, or influence clinician behavior indirectly, making oversight more complex than for static technologies.

Regulators must balance two competing imperatives: enabling innovation that improves care, while preventing unsafe, biased, or unvalidated technologies from entering clinical practice. As a result, regulatory agencies worldwide are adapting existing medical device frameworks to accommodate AI.

The Role of the U.S. Food and Drug Administration (FDA)

In the United States, the Food and Drug Administration (FDA) is the primary authority responsible for regulating medical devices, including AI-enabled systems used in healthcare. The FDA evaluates whether a product is safe and effective for its intended use before it can be marketed.

AI-based healthcare products are typically regulated through one of several pathways:

- 510(k) clearance, which requires demonstrating substantial equivalence to an existing approved device
- De Novo classification, for novel, low-to-moderate risk devices without a predicate
- Premarket approval (PMA), for high-risk devices requiring extensive clinical evidence

The FDA has been particularly active in developing guidance on AI and machine-learning-based software. It recognizes that traditional regulatory models, designed for static devices, are not fully suited to adaptive algorithms. As a result, the FDA has proposed a lifecycle-based regulatory approach that emphasizes continuous monitoring, post-market surveillance, and real-world performance evaluation.

For example, an AI algorithm designed to detect diabetic retinopathy from retinal images must demonstrate diagnostic accuracy, robustness across populations, and safe integration into clinical workflows before approval.

The European Medicines Agency (EMA) and EU Frameworks

In the European Union, healthcare AI is regulated under a combination of medical device regulations and data protection laws. The European Medicines Agency (EMA) plays a role in regulating medicinal products, while AI-enabled medical devices fall under the EU Medical Device Regulation (MDR).

The MDR introduces stricter requirements for:

- Clinical evaluation
- Risk management
- Post-market surveillance
- Transparency and traceability

In parallel, the EU has proposed the AI Act, a comprehensive regulatory framework that classifies AI systems by risk. High-risk AI systems, including many healthcare applications, are subject to enhanced requirements around data quality, transparency, human oversight, and accountability.

Together, these frameworks reflect the EU's emphasis on precaution, patient rights, and ethical governance.

The Central Drugs Standard Control Organization (CDSCO)

In India, the Central Drugs Standard Control Organization (CDSCO) regulates medical devices and pharmaceuticals. While India's AI-specific healthcare regulations are still evolving, AI-enabled medical software increasingly falls under the country's medical device rules.

CDSCO's approach emphasizes:

- Risk classification of medical software
- Clinical evaluation and performance validation
- Compliance with quality management standards
- Post-market surveillance and reporting

As India rapidly expands digital health infrastructure, including national health data platforms, regulatory clarity around AI is becoming increasingly important. CDSCO is expected to align more closely with international standards while addressing India's unique healthcare scale and diversity.

Software as a Medical Device (SaMD)

Software as a Medical Device (SaMD) refers to software intended to perform a medical function without being part of a physical medical device. Many AI systems in healthcare fall into this category, including diagnostic algorithms, clinical decision support tools, and predictive analytics platforms.

SaMD may:

- Diagnose disease
- Recommend treatment options
- Predict clinical risk
- Monitor disease progression

The classification of AI as SaMD is critical because it determines regulatory obligations, validation requirements, and oversight mechanisms.

Risk-Based Classification of SaMD

Global regulators increasingly adopt a risk-based approach to SaMD. Risk is determined by:

- The severity of the clinical condition addressed
- The significance of the information provided by the software
- Whether the software informs or drives clinical decisions

For example:

- A wellness app that tracks steps may be low risk
- A diagnostic AI that detects cancer from imaging is high risk

Higher-risk SaMD requires more rigorous clinical evidence, validation, and monitoring.

Clinical Evaluation of AI-Based SaMD

Clinical evaluation for SaMD focuses on demonstrating:

- Analytical validity (does the algorithm function as intended?)
- Clinical validity (does it accurately predict or detect disease?)
- Clinical utility (does it improve outcomes or decision-making?)

Unlike traditional devices, AI systems must also demonstrate robustness across populations, imaging devices, and clinical settings. Regulators increasingly expect evidence that AI performs safely in real-world conditions, not just controlled datasets.

Adaptive Algorithms and Regulatory Challenges

One of the most complex issues in SaMD regulation is adaptive AI, systems that continue learning after deployment. Continuous learning challenges traditional approval models, which assume fixed functionality.

To address this, regulators are exploring frameworks that allow:

- Predefined algorithm change protocols
- Ongoing performance monitoring
- Controlled updates with regulatory oversight

This represents a shift from one-time approval toward continuous regulatory engagement.

Certification, Audits, and Compliance

Regulatory approval is only one component of compliance. Healthcare AI developers and deployers must also maintain robust quality management systems (QMS). These systems ensure that products are developed, tested, maintained, and updated according to defined standards.

Common QMS standards include:

- ISO 13485 for medical devices
- ISO 62304 for medical software lifecycle processes
- ISO 14971 for risk management

A strong QMS demonstrates organizational maturity and commitment to safety.

Audits and Regulatory Inspections

Regulatory authorities may conduct audits to verify compliance with approved processes and standards. Audits assess:

- Data governance practices
- Model validation procedures
- Change management controls
- Post-market surveillance systems

For healthcare organizations deploying AI, audits also examine how tools are used in practice, including clinician training, documentation, and escalation protocols.

Post-Market Surveillance and Monitoring

AI systems require continuous oversight after deployment. Post-market surveillance involves:

- Monitoring real-world performance
- Tracking adverse events or near misses
- Detecting performance drift or bias
- Updating models responsibly

Regulators increasingly expect healthcare organizations to treat AI as a living system rather than a static product.

Documentation and Traceability

Compliance depends heavily on documentation. Organizations must maintain clear records of:

- Training data sources
- Model versions and updates
- Validation results
- Deployment configurations
- Decision logs and audit trails

Traceability supports accountability, safety investigations, and regulatory reporting.

Global Harmonization Efforts

Healthcare AI development is global, but regulation remains largely national. Fragmented regulatory requirements increase costs, slow innovation, and create barriers to equitable access.

Global harmonization efforts aim to:

- Reduce duplication of regulatory work
- Establish common safety and performance principles
- Enable cross-border deployment of trusted AI systems

International Medical Device Regulators Forum (IMDRF)

The IMDRF plays a central role in aligning global regulatory approaches to medical devices, including SaMD. Its guidance documents define:

- Risk categorization frameworks
- Clinical evaluation principles
- Quality management expectations

Many national regulators, including the FDA and EMA, align their policies with IMDRF guidance.

Toward Common AI Governance Principles

Beyond device regulation, global organizations are working to establish shared ethical and governance principles for AI. These efforts emphasize:

- Human oversight
- Transparency and explainability
- Fairness and non-discrimination
- Accountability and safety

While implementation varies, convergence around core principles supports trust and interoperability.

Challenges to Harmonization

Despite progress, harmonization faces challenges:

- Differing legal systems and healthcare models
- Variability in data protection laws
- Uneven technical and regulatory capacity across countries

Balancing global alignment with local context remains a central tension.

Conclusion

Regulatory frameworks and standards are foundational to the responsible deployment of AI in healthcare. Far from stifling innovation, effective regulation creates the conditions under which AI can be trusted, scaled, and sustained.

As AI systems become more adaptive and influential, regulation must evolve toward lifecycle-based oversight, continuous monitoring, and global collaboration. Healthcare organizations that understand and engage proactively with regulatory frameworks will be better positioned to harness the benefits of AI while protecting patients, clinicians, and society.

The final chapter looks ahead to emerging trends and future directions, exploring how AI may continue to reshape healthcare in the years to come.

Part IV

Future Directions

Chapter 16: Emerging Trends and Technologies in Artificial Intelligence for Healthcare

Artificial intelligence in healthcare is no longer confined to pattern recognition or decision support. As computational capabilities, data availability, and algorithmic sophistication continue to advance, AI is beginning to reshape not only how care is delivered, but how health systems anticipate disease, design therapies, and understand the human body itself.

The next generation of healthcare AI extends beyond optimization of existing workflows toward fundamentally new models of care, discovery, and prevention.

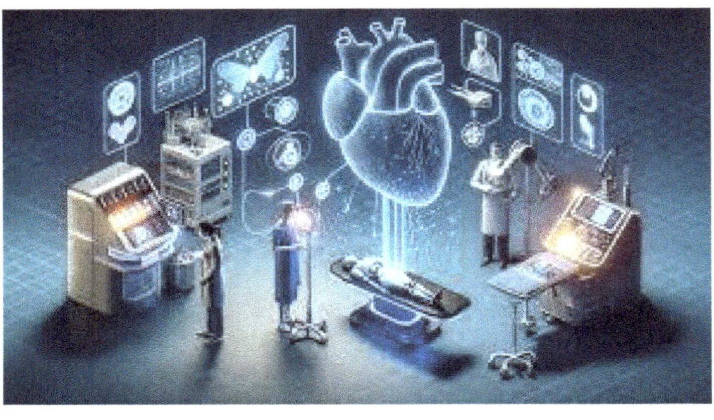

This chapter explores five major emerging trends that are likely to define the future of AI in healthcare: generative AI in clinical practice, digital twins and simulation, brain–computer interfaces, predictive public health and pandemic preparedness, and AI-driven drug discovery and clinical trials.

Together, these developments signal a shift from reactive, episodic care toward predictive, personalized, and system-level intelligence.

Generative AI in Clinical Practice

Traditional healthcare AI has focused primarily on classification, prediction, and detection, identifying disease, estimating risk, or flagging abnormalities. Generative AI represents a qualitative shift. Rather than simply analyzing existing data, generative models produce new outputs, including text, images, summaries, recommendations, and simulations.

In clinical practice, generative AI systems can synthesize information across multiple sources and generate context-aware responses. This capability positions generative AI as a potential interface layer between clinicians, patients, and complex medical data.

Clinical Documentation and Knowledge Synthesis

One of the earliest and most impactful applications of generative AI is clinical documentation. Generative systems can draft progress notes, discharge summaries, referral letters, and patient instructions based on clinical conversations and structured data. Unlike rule-based templates, these systems adapt language and structure to the clinical context.

Beyond documentation, generative AI assists clinicians in synthesizing large volumes of medical information. For example, a system may summarize a patient's longitudinal history, highlight key changes, and generate a concise clinical narrative that supports decision-making. This reduces cognitive load and helps clinicians focus on interpretation rather than information retrieval.

Decision Support and Clinical Reasoning Assistance

Generative AI is increasingly used to support clinical reasoning. By integrating guidelines, evidence, and patient-specific data, generative systems can propose differential diagnoses, suggest diagnostic workups, or outline treatment options. Importantly, these outputs are probabilistic and exploratory rather than definitive.

In complex cases involving multimorbidity, generative AI can help clinicians reason through competing priorities by articulating trade-offs, risks, and potential outcomes. This supports deliberative decision-making rather than automated conclusions.

Patient Communication and Education

Generative AI also enhances patient engagement by translating clinical information into understandable, personalized explanations. Systems can generate educational content tailored to a patient's diagnosis, literacy level, and cultural context, improving comprehension and adherence.

However, the use of generative AI in clinical practice raises important concerns around accuracy, hallucination, accountability, and trust. These systems must be deployed with rigorous safeguards, human oversight, and clear boundaries regarding the scope of use.

Digital Twins and Simulation

A digital twin is a computational representation of a real-world system that updates dynamically as new data arrives. In healthcare, digital twins model individual patients, organs, or physiological systems, allowing clinicians and researchers to simulate disease progression and treatment response in silico.

Unlike static risk models, digital twins evolve over time, incorporating new clinical data, behavioral information, and environmental factors. This enables continuous personalization and scenario testing.

Patient-Level Digital Twins

At the individual level, digital twins integrate data from electronic health records, imaging, genomics, wearables, and patient-reported outcomes to create a living model of a patient's health. Clinicians can simulate how different interventions, such as medications, surgeries, and lifestyle changes, might affect outcomes.

For example, in cardiovascular care, a digital twin may model blood flow, plaque progression, and hemodynamic response to therapy. In oncology, digital twins may simulate tumor growth and response to different treatment regimens, supporting personalized planning.

Organ and System-Level Simulation

Digital twins are also used at the organ or system level. Virtual heart models simulate electrical conduction and mechanical contraction, supporting arrhythmia treatment planning. Musculoskeletal digital twins help optimize orthopedic implants or rehabilitation strategies.

At a broader level, hospital or health system digital twins simulate patient flow, resource utilization, and capacity constraints. These models support operational planning, surge response, and infrastructure investment decisions.

Ethical and Practical Considerations

While digital twins offer powerful predictive capabilities, they rely on assumptions and incomplete data. Overconfidence in simulations can create false certainty. Transparency about model limitations, uncertainty, and validation is essential to responsible use.

Brain-Computer Interfaces

Brain–computer interfaces (BCIs) enable direct communication between the brain and external devices by translating neural signals into actionable outputs. Advances in AI have accelerated BCI development by improving signal decoding, noise reduction, and adaptive learning.

In healthcare, BCIs are primarily explored for restoring function, augmenting communication, and supporting rehabilitation in patients with neurological impairment.

Clinical Applications of BCIs

BCIs have demonstrated promise in enabling communication for individuals with paralysis or advanced neurodegenerative disease. AI algorithms decode neural signals associated with intended speech or movement, allowing patients to control cursors, generate text, or operate assistive devices.

In rehabilitation, BCIs support neuroplasticity by providing real-time feedback during motor recovery. Patients recovering from stroke, for example, may use BCIs to reinforce brain–muscle connections through guided therapy.

Ethical and Societal Implications

BCIs raise profound ethical questions around autonomy, identity, privacy, and consent. Neural data is deeply personal, and misuse could have significant consequences. Governance frameworks must address data ownership, long-term monitoring, and psychological impact.

As BCIs move closer to mainstream clinical use, ethical safeguards must evolve alongside technical capability.

Predictive Public Health and Pandemic Preparedness

Traditional public health surveillance relies on retrospective data, such as case counts, hospitalizations, and mortality reports. AI enables a shift toward predictive public health by analyzing diverse, real-time data sources to anticipate outbreaks and system stress.

These sources include clinical data, environmental signals, mobility patterns, social media trends, and genomic surveillance.

Early Warning Systems

AI-driven early warning systems detect anomalies that may signal emerging threats. For example, increases in respiratory symptoms, over-the-counter medication purchases, or wastewater viral markers may precede confirmed outbreaks.

By identifying patterns earlier, public health authorities can intervene sooner, reducing transmission and impact.

Resource Planning and Response Optimization

During health emergencies, AI models support dynamic allocation of resources such as hospital beds, ventilators, vaccines, and personnel. Simulation models help decision-makers evaluate policy options, such as travel restrictions or vaccination strategies, under uncertainty.

The COVID-19 pandemic demonstrated both the potential and limitations of AI in public health. Future preparedness depends on better data integration, transparency, and trust.

AI in Drug Discovery and Clinical Trials

Drug discovery is traditionally slow, expensive, and high-risk. AI is transforming this process by accelerating target identification, molecule design, and candidate optimization.

Machine learning models analyze biological pathways, protein structures, and chemical libraries to identify promising compounds. Generative models design novel molecules with desired properties, reducing reliance on brute-force screening.

Precision Clinical Trials

AI is also reshaping clinical trials by improving patient selection, trial design, and outcome prediction. Predictive models identify patients most likely to respond to a therapy, improving trial efficiency and reducing failure rates.

AI-driven monitoring of trial data enables early detection of safety signals or efficacy trends, supporting adaptive trial designs.

Ethical and Regulatory Considerations

While AI accelerates discovery, it also introduces new ethical and regulatory challenges. Transparency, reproducibility, and validation remain essential, particularly when AI-generated molecules move toward human testing.

Conclusion

The emerging trends explored in this chapter reflect a broader evolution in healthcare AI - from tools that assist clinicians to systems that model, simulate, and anticipate health at individual and population levels. Generative AI, digital twins, BCIs, predictive public health, and AI-driven drug discovery each expand the scope of what is possible.

Yet, technological capability alone is insufficient. The future of AI in healthcare depends on responsible governance, ethical design, clinical integration, and societal trust. When aligned with human values and health system priorities, these emerging technologies offer the potential to transform healthcare from reactive treatment to proactive, personalized, and resilient care systems.

Conclusion: Realizing the Promise of AI in Healthcare

Artificial intelligence has moved decisively from the periphery of healthcare innovation to its strategic core. What was once viewed as experimental, speculative, or narrowly technical has now become deeply embedded in how health systems think about prevention, diagnosis, treatment, monitoring, and population health.

This book has traced that transformation from foundational concepts and core technologies to real-world applications, ethical considerations, governance frameworks, and emerging frontiers.

Across its chapters, one central insight has remained constant: AI is not a single tool or solution, but a new layer of intelligence that reshapes how healthcare systems learn, adapt, and deliver care. Its impact depends not only on algorithmic sophistication but on how thoughtfully it is designed, integrated, governed, and aligned with human values.

Reframing Healthcare as an Information System

At its core, healthcare is an information-driven endeavor. Every clinical encounter produces data, including symptoms, images, laboratory results, narratives, behaviors, and outcomes. Historically, the ability to convert this data into timely, actionable insight has been constrained by human cognitive limits, fragmented systems, and episodic models of care.

Artificial intelligence fundamentally alters this equation. As explored in the early chapters of this book, AI enables healthcare systems to process vast, heterogeneous data streams at scale, uncover patterns invisible to human perception, and support decisions under uncertainty. Machine learning, deep learning, natural language processing, computer vision, and predictive analytics are not abstract technologies; they are the engines that allow modern healthcare to function in the face of rising complexity, aging populations, chronic disease burden, and workforce constraints.

Importantly, this book emphasizes that AI does not replace clinical reasoning; it augments it. The most effective systems do not automate medicine. Rather, they enhance human judgment by reducing noise, improving consistency, and extending clinical insight beyond the limits of time and attention.

From Episodic Care to Continuous, Preventive Models

A recurring theme throughout this book is the shift from episodic, reactive care to continuous, proactive health management. Wearables, remote monitoring, symptom checkers, and virtual assistants extend care beyond clinic walls, capturing real-world data that reflects how people actually live between visits.

AI-driven monitoring systems detect early signs of deterioration, personalize alerts, and support timely intervention, often before symptoms escalate into emergencies. In chronic disease management, this capability is transformative. Conditions that once progressed silently until irreversible damage occurred can now be identified earlier, managed more dynamically, and monitored more safely at scale.

This transition reframes healthcare not as a series of isolated encounters, but as an ongoing relationship supported by intelligent systems. Prevention, early detection, and long-term engagement become achievable goals rather than aspirational ideals.

Precision Without Dehumanization

One of the greatest promises as well as risks of AI in healthcare is personalization. This book illustrates how AI enables more precise alignment between interventions and individual patient needs.

Yet precision alone is not enough. This book has consistently argued that personalization must remain human-centered. AI systems can stratify risk, simulate outcomes, and recommend options - but they cannot define values, priorities, or meaning. Shared decision-making, empathy, and ethical judgment remain essential.

The most successful AI-enabled care models are those that use precision to support dignity: reducing trial-and-error treatments, minimizing unnecessary burden, and aligning care with what matters most to patients - not merely what is statistically optimal.

Scaling Expertise Without Eroding Trust

Healthcare systems around the world face profound capacity challenges. Shortages of clinicians, uneven access to specialists, and growing demand threaten sustainability. AI offers a powerful way to scale expertise, supporting triage, diagnostics, surgical planning, emergency care, and population health management.

However, scale without trust is fragile. As explored in chapters on ethics, regulation, data governance, and implementation strategy, trust is not a byproduct of technological success. Instead, it is an outcome of transparency, accountability, and responsible design.

Bias, explainability, consent, privacy, cybersecurity, and regulatory compliance are not peripheral concerns. They determine whether AI systems are adopted, relied upon, and sustained. This book has emphasized that responsible AI is not slower innovation - it is durable innovation.

Integration, Not Invention, Is the Hardest Problem

A recurring lesson across chapters is that the hardest challenges in healthcare AI are not technical, but organizational. Integration into clinical workflows, alignment with reimbursement models, training of the workforce, and change management determine whether AI delivers real value or remains confined to pilots and proofs of concept.

AI succeeds when it fits naturally into how clinicians work, when it reduces friction rather than adds burden, and when it respects professional autonomy. It fails when it demands parallel systems, excessive data entry, or blind trust.

Implementation, therefore, is not an afterthought - it is a core competency. Health systems that invest in readiness assessments, multidisciplinary governance, evaluation metrics, and iterative scaling are best positioned to realize the benefits of AI.

Emerging Technologies and the Next Horizon

The final chapters of this book looked forward to generative AI, digital twins, brain-computer interfaces, predictive public health, and AI-driven drug discovery. These technologies point toward a future in which healthcare becomes increasingly anticipatory, simulated, and adaptive.

Digital twins suggest a world where clinicians can test interventions before applying them. Generative AI hints at new interfaces between humans and medical knowledge. Predictive public health offers the possibility of responding to crises before they unfold. AI-accelerated drug discovery holds promise for faster, more targeted therapies.

Yet these advances also heighten ethical stakes. As AI systems grow more powerful, the need for governance, humility, and human oversight becomes even more critical. The future of healthcare AI is not about replacing clinicians or automating care - it is about building systems that learn responsibly and serve collectively defined goals.

A Hopeful but Grounded Future

The future outlined in this book is neither utopian nor dystopian. It is complex, conditional, and deeply human. Artificial intelligence will not solve every problem in healthcare - but when deployed thoughtfully, it can meaningfully improve outcomes, equity, efficiency, and experience.

The most hopeful vision is not one of machines making decisions for humans, but of healthcare systems that learn continuously, support clinicians rather than exhaust them, and extend care to those who have historically been underserved.

Realizing this future requires collaboration across disciplines: clinicians, patients, technologists, policymakers, ethicists, and educators. It requires moving beyond hype toward evidence, beyond silos toward integration, and beyond short-term gains toward long-term stewardship.

Closing Reflection

Artificial intelligence is often described as transformative - but transformation is not automatic. It is shaped by choices: what we build, how we deploy it, whom it serves, and how we govern it.

This book has sought to provide not only an explanation of AI in healthcare but a framework for engaging with it responsibly. Understanding the technology is necessary - but not sufficient. What matters most is how intelligence is translated into impact, and whether that impact advances a healthcare system that is more humane, more equitable, and more resilient than the one we have today.

If artificial intelligence is to fulfill its promise in healthcare, it must ultimately help us do what medicine has always aspired to do: see patients more clearly, act earlier and more wisely, and care more consistently for both individuals and populations.

When guided by these principles, the future of AI in healthcare is not something to fear - but something to shape, deliberately and together.